W9-CBE-964

TENURE DENIED

CASES OF SEX DISCRIMINATION
IN ACADEMIA

A AUW Educational Foundation
AAUW Legal Advocacy Fund

Published by the American Association of University Women Educational Foundation
and the American Association of University Women Legal Advocacy Fund
1111 Sixteenth St. N.W.
Washington, DC 20036
Phone: 202/728-7602
Fax: 202/463-7169
TDD: 202/785-7777
E-mail: foundation@aauw.org
Web: www.aauw.org

First printing: October 2004
Editor: Susan K. Dyer
Graphic designer: Kenneth Krattenmaker
Cover design: Emily D. Goward

Library of Congress Control Number: 2004113560
ISBN: 1-879922-34-7

If you have questions about this report, contact the AAUW Legal Advocacy Fund
at 202/785-7750 or laf@aauw.org or the AAUW Educational Foundation at
202/728-7602 or foundation@aauw.org.

010-05 7K 10/04

Table of Contents

Foreword

Too often, women who file charges of sex discrimination are stereotyped as humorless people who can't take a joke or overly sensitive individuals who pursue lawsuits for personal gain. *Tenure Denied: Cases of Sex Discrimination in Academia* presents evidence that belies these stereotypes and gives a human voice to the concept of sex discrimination in academia. As this report makes clear, professors-turned-litigants are spurred by significantly more than an off-color joke or an occasional slight. Plaintiffs have risked and sometimes sacrificed promising, prestigious academic careers to seek justice for themselves and other women.

Since the early 1980s, the American Association of University Women Legal Advocacy Fund has supported women faculty members in more than 60 cases of sex discrimination in higher education. Many have become important cases in the development and interpretation of Title VII of the Civil Rights Act of 1964 and other sex discrimination law. *Tenure Denied* draws from this unique archive of cases to assess the phenomenon of sex discrimination for female faculty at the height of their careers and to learn what actually happens to women on campus and in court.

Discrimination in the tenure process is not just a women's issue nor is it solely an academic issue. Colleges and universities hold an exulted place in U.S. society, and tenured professors occupy an esteemed status within these institutions. Because employers require a college degree for most better-paying jobs (and by doing so, essentially depend on the performance and judgment of university faculty when selecting employees), achieving diversity among the powerful ranks of tenured professors is an important issue for everyone.

In the end, the court of public opinion may prove most important. Universities and colleges do not want to be seen as unfair by parents, alumni, students, or potential students. And our increasingly diverse population will demand that higher education institutions use the full talents of all—regardless of gender.

AAUW is proud of its commitment to equitable hiring and tenure practices in academia and of the support that the Legal Advocacy Fund has provided to women faculty. We hope this report furthers awareness of sex discrimination in academia and serves as a springboard for the development and implementation of fair and equitable tenure processes at universities and colleges nationwide.

Mary Ellen Smyth

Mary Ellen Smyth
President
AAUW Educational Foundation

Michele Warholic Wetherald

Michele Warholic Wetherald
President
AAUW Legal Advocacy Fund

October 2004

The **American Association of University Women** is one of the nation's leading voices promoting education and equity for women and girls.

The **AAUW Educational Foundation** is a leader in research on the educational and economic status of women and girls. One of the world's largest sources of funding exclusively for women pursuing graduate degrees, the Educational Foundation supports aspiring scholars around the globe, teachers and activists in local communities, women at critical stages of their careers, and those pursuing professions where women are underrepresented.

The **AAUW Legal Advocacy Fund** is the nation's only legal fund focused solely on the elimination of sex discrimination in higher education. LAF provides financial support to women litigating sex discrimination cases, offers a nationwide referral network of lawyers and experts, educates campuses and communities about discriminatory barriers facing women in higher education, and rewards campus programs that demonstrate progress toward equity.

Acknowledgments

AAUW gratefully acknowledges the hard work, support, and contributions of the many people involved in the initiation, development, and production of this publication.

Pamela Haag deserves appreciation for shaping and conducting the research for this report. Elena Silva and Catherine Hill of the AAUW Educational Foundation and Leslie T. Annexstein of the AAUW Legal Advocacy Fund wrote the report based on Haag's original manuscript. They were assisted by LAF staff member Marika Dunn and LAF interns Erica Boshes-Feldman and Tamara Wallace. AAUW staff member Sue Dyer edited the report, contributing in terms of substance as well as style.

Special thanks to AAUW of Pennsylvania, which generously supported this project through its 75th-anniversary Diamond Donor campaign. While many individuals and branches contributed to this campaign, AAUW especially thanks those individuals at the Diamond Donor level: Jerry Blum, Arlene Butts, Sally Chamberlain, Doris Cohen, Wendy Armour Dickinson, Marjorie Dunaway, Barbara Gold, Kathy Lepovetsky, Don Mowery, Marjorie Mowery, Susan Nenstiel, Virginia Palmer, Karen Rowe, Patricia Sand, Linda Tozier, and Sue Zitnick.

Finally, AAUW offers sincere gratitude to the Legal Advocacy Fund–supported plaintiffs whose stories are included here. Their experiences leading up to and throughout their lawsuits shed light on the nature of sex discrimination and the character of tenure review in academia. AAUW thanks them for their courage in coming forward with their stories. AAUW also thanks the many attorneys and other professionals who assisted these plaintiffs.

Abbreviations

AAUP	American Association of University Professors
AAUW	American Association of University Women
EEOC	U.S. Equal Employment Opportunity Commission
F.2d, F.3d	*Federal Reporter* (opinions of the U.S. Circuit Courts of Appeals)
F. Supp.	*Federal Supplement* (opinions of the U.S. District Courts)
LAF	AAUW Legal Advocacy Fund
Title VII	Title VII of the Civil Rights Act of 1964
Title IX	Title IX of the Education Amendments of 1972
U.S.	*United States Reports* (opinions of the U.S. Supreme Court)
U.S.C.	United States Code
WL	Westlaw

Definitions

Certiorari – Appeal to the U.S. Supreme Court

Collegiality – Collaboration and cooperation among colleagues

Discovery – Part of the pretrial litigation process during which each party requests relevant information and documents from the other side in an attempt to "discover" pertinent facts. Discovery devices include depositions, interrogatories, or requests for documents and other information

Disparate impact discrimination – Employment policies or practices that appear neutral on their face but that result in discrimination against a protected group

Disparate treatment discrimination – Differential treatment of employees or applicants on the basis of their protected status, such as sex

En banc – Court sessions in which all of the judges participate rather than the usual quorum

Mixed motives – Motives that are both legitimate and discriminatory

Pretext – Ostensible reason or motive given as a cover for the real reason or motive

Prima facie – A case that at first glance presents sufficient evidence for the plaintiff to win and thus allows the case to go forward

Similarly situated – Professors who have similar qualifications for teaching, scholarship, or service and can be compared to assess discrimination

Summary judgment – Procedural device available to any party when she or he believes that no genuine issue of material fact exists and that she or he is entitled to prevail as a matter of law

Tenure – Promise of lifetime employment awarded to professors who demonstrate excellence in scholarship, teaching, and service

CHAPTER 1

Introduction

During the last two decades, women have made remarkable strides in academia: They are graduating from colleges and universities in record numbers and making striking gains in doctoral programs. In academic year 2000–01, for example, women made up 44 percent of doctoral recipients, up from 32 percent in 1980–81 (see Appendix A, Table 1). In the 1980s and 1990s, women also made impressive gains in faculty appointments at all ranks, growing from about one-fourth of the full-time faculty to more than one-third (see Appendix A, Table 2).

On average, compared to men, women earn less, hold lower-ranking positions, and are less likely to have tenure.

Despite these gains, women remain underrepresented at the highest echelons of higher education. Women make up more than one-half of instructors and lecturers and nearly one-half of assistant professors, but they represent only one-third of associate professors and one-fifth of full professors (see Appendix A, Table 2). On average, compared to men, women earn less, hold lower-ranking positions, and are less likely to have tenure.[1] For four-year institutions, the differences are more pronounced (see Appendix A, Table 3).

---

[1] Full and associate professors are most likely to hold tenure. In academic year 1999–2000, for example, 95 percent of full professors, 83 percent of associate professors, 14 percent of assistant professors, 3 percent of instructors, and 2 percent of lecturers held tenure (U.S. Department of Education 2002, Table 242).

This report focuses on women who took their fight for tenure to the courts. Drawing on 19 cases supported by the American Association of University Women Legal Advocacy Fund since 1981, we document the challenge of fighting sex discrimination in academia. In the process, we illustrate the overt and subtle forms of sex discrimination that continue to bar women from tenure, the most venerated and secure status of academia.

Sex discrimination in tenure decisions is not just unfair; it also has repercussions in the workplace and in society in general. Universities and colleges have been powerful cultural institutions in western culture since medieval times. Today, the college degree has become the standard credential used by employers to screen applicants for most better-paying jobs. Tenured faculty control curriculum and grading and, in so doing, play a central role in determining this credential. As teachers and mentors, professors help shape the intellect and social conscience of their students and, hence, of our society. Offering students a faculty as diverse as the world they live in and ensuring the fairness of the promotion process is thus of tremendous importance.

In academia as in the rest of the workplace, female workers are now commonplace. Women expect to work throughout their lives, and a majority of women work for pay even when their children are infants and toddlers. So far women have not achieved parity in positions of leadership, and they are still underrepresented in upper management and high-paying jobs throughout the work force, despite the fact that more women have professional degrees. The burgeoning pipeline of women professors with doctorates has yet to translate into full gender equity among tenured faculty. As the stories described in this report demonstrate, sex discrimination remains a critical part of the problem.

What Is Tenure?

Tenure is a promise of lifetime employment awarded to scholars who demonstrate excellence in scholarship, teaching, and service. According to the landmark *Statement of Principles on Academic*

Freedom and Tenure made in 1940 by the American Association of University Professors and the Association of American Colleges, tenured faculty can be fired "only for adequate cause, except in the case of retirement for age, or under extraordinary circumstances because of financial exigencies." The burden of proof for adequate cause or financial exigencies rests with the university or college, and dismissal of tenured faculty is rare. Tenure conveys the approval of the academic community as a whole and ushers the fortunate candidate into a job with extraordinary job security and prestige.

Tenure review generally takes place five to seven years after a candidate is hired. Although the nature of tenure review varies greatly, the criteria for tenure generally include research, teaching, and service. Most tenure committees depend on their own judgments, evaluations from outside faculty with expertise in the candidate's area, and student evaluations or other forms of student input. Typically, the candidate's department manages the process and makes the initial recommendation to the dean. In most cases, but not always, the final decision maker—the provost or board of trustees—will defer to the dean's recommendation.

A negative tenure decision is always painful. Losing a bid for tenure is much more damaging than being passed over for a promotion because the rejected candidate usually loses her or his job and must leave the university by the next academic year. Because academic disciplines are often tightly knit communities, rejected faculty can find it difficult to get a new job elsewhere in academia. Some faculty are able to continue their careers but only in schools that are considered less prestigious or that offer fewer resources. In disciplines where few jobs are available outside of the academic context, many rejected tenure candidates are forced to change careers altogether—a difficult, time-consuming, and often costly feat. While universities and colleges stress the permanent nature of the tenure contract, they often gloss over the fact that a negative tenure decision terminates the candidate's job and, sometimes, her or his career.

The tenure process has a number of characteristics that contribute to the likelihood that the matter will end up in court. In a typical case, the tenure file and committee proceedings are confidential. Secrecy is needed, some argue, to allow for candid review. The downside, however, is that candidates do not have access to key documents used to make the tenure decision and often learn about deliberations through rumor. Because candidates receive only partial or inaccurate information, they do not know if they have been treated fairly.

Ambiguity about the standards needed to secure tenure can be another point of contention for many rejected candidates. Universities do not have straightforward publication or teaching standards that guarantee tenure. As a plaintiff highlighted in this report learned, several books and dozens of peer-reviewed articles do not always result in tenure. Disagreement even exists about how to "count" articles or books. Within a discipline, the prestige of a particular journal or kind of scholarship can be subject to debate. For example, an article in a women's studies journal is sometimes viewed as a "second tier" publication compared to a publication in a traditional discipline, even if the women's studies journal has wide circulation and a good reputation among interested scholars.

> Biased behavior and decision making remain a serious problem in the promotion and tenure processes of many universities and colleges.

While the standards for granting tenure remain ambiguous in the eyes of many applicants, most academics agree that standards have risen during the 1980s and 1990s as the number of tenure-track and tenured positions has dwindled relative to the number of applicants. This belief is so widely held that, as one judge noted in the *Hirschhorn v. University of Kentucky* case described in Chapter 2, a tenured professor usually cannot be used as a point of comparison for a tenure candidate because the standards have risen so substantially. Ironically, some of the older tenured faculty presiding over tenure cases would not receive tenure by today's competitive standards. This discrepancy can exacerbate the frustration of rejected tenure candidates and raise questions of fair treatment.

Biased behavior and decision making remain a serious problem in the promotion and tenure processes of many universities and colleges. In some cases described herein, discrimination was overt. For example, one department chair argued that a woman professor didn't need her job as much as a man did because she was married (and presumably could depend on her husband for support). In other cases, discrimination was more subtle, manifesting itself in the guise of personal animosity toward a female professor who did not seem sufficiently "collegial." Either way, if evidence indicates that tenure was denied based on gender, the candidate can sue the university for sex discrimination.

The AAUW Legal Advocacy Fund

Filing a complaint of sex discrimination for denial of tenure and litigating that case are not easy tasks. A plaintiff must have capable and committed counsel, compelling facts, emotional strength, and a will of steel. The AAUW Legal Advocacy Fund provides support to women seeking legal redress for sex discrimination in higher education. Founded in 1981, LAF is the nation's only legal fund focused solely on eliminating sex discrimination in higher education. It has helped female students, faculty, employees, and administrators challenge discriminatory practices such as sexual harassment, pay inequity, denial of tenure and promotions, retaliation for complaining about discrimination, and inequality in women's athletics programs. In addition to providing financial support, LAF offers a legal resource referral network of attorneys and experts who consult with women, provides education programs on sex discrimination on campus and for the public, and rewards campus programs that promote gender equity.

The case *Zahorik v. Cornell University*, 579 F. Supp. 349 (N.D.N.Y. 1983) was the impetus for the creation of the Legal Advocacy Fund. Eleven women faculty and coaches brought a complaint of sex discrimination against Cornell University alleging violations of both Title VII of the Civil Rights Act of 1964 and Title IX of the

Education Amendments of 1972. To support the plaintiffs, members of the Ithaca, New York, branch of AAUW joined forces with a group known as the Friends of the Cornell 11. The Ithaca branch members asked AAUW to bank funds raised in support of the plaintiffs' case, and LAF was born.

Although the focus in this report is on sex discrimination, cases that include discrimination based on race, age, or disability in addition to sex are a growing part of LAF's portfolio, presenting new challenges in understanding and tackling gender inequity and bias in academia. For statistics on faculty by race and ethnicity, see Appendix A, Table 4. For further information on the cases LAF supports, visit the AAUW website at www.aauw.org.

Sex Discrimination Laws and Judicial Interpretation

Most of the tenure denial cases filed in federal court are brought under Title VII of the Civil Rights Act of 1964, which prohibits discrimination on the basis of sex, race, national origin, and religion in employment.[2] Discrimination based on sex was not initially covered under Title VII. Gender was added as a last minute amendment by a conservative congressman intent on killing the bill. A small group of female legislators successfully rallied to support the amendment, and discrimination based on sex was included. From this awkward beginning, lawyers and plaintiffs have tried to build a coherent legal defense against sex discrimination.[3]

Two approaches to sex discrimination litigation exist under Title VII and have been developed through court decisions. The first major U.S. Supreme Court Title VII case, *Griggs v. Duke Power Company*, 401 U.S. 424 (1971), applied a "disparate impact" theory

---

[2] As originally enacted, Title VII did not cover faculty members at universities and colleges. Spurred by discrimination in educational institutions, Congress amended Title VII in 1972 to cover faculty at these institutions. Title IX of the Education Amendments of 1972 was also passed to prohibit sex discrimination in education programs or activities receiving federal funds. While most sex discrimination in tenure cases have been filed under Title VII, and this is the primary law discussed throughout this report, Title IX also covers employees of educational institutions.

of employment discrimination under Title VII. Disparate impact discrimination refers to practices that appear neutral on their face but that result in discrimination against a protected group. The issue in *Griggs* was whether an employer could require job applicants to have a high school diploma and pass aptitude tests that, the plaintiffs argued, were not based on real job requirements. Because these requirements excluded a much larger percentage of African American men than white men, the plaintiffs argued that the requirements constituted disparate impact discrimination. While the tenure process appears to exclude a larger percentage of women than men, few tenure cases alleging sex discrimination have proceeded under the disparate impact theory.[4]

Most cases of sex discrimination in tenure denial have proceeded under a second approach: the theory of "disparate treatment," which refers to the differential treatment of employees or applicants on the basis of their race, color, religion, sex, or national origin. Under this approach, a plaintiff must prove intentional discrimination using direct or circumstantial evidence. The Supreme Court articulated the framework for proving disparate treatment discrimination in the landmark decision in *McDonnell Douglas Corporation v. Green*, 411 U.S. 792 (1973). Under *McDonnell Douglas*, the plaintiff must first establish a prima facie case by showing that she (1) belongs to a protected class, (2) is qualified for the position, (3) suffered an adverse employment action, and (4) was replaced with someone outside the protected class, i.e., a male. A plaintiff may meet the fourth element by showing that a comparable nonprotected person was treated more favorably.

---

[3] Women denied tenure also may claim violations of the Pregnancy Discrimination Act. The Pregnancy Discrimination Act is an amendment to Title VII and prohibits discrimination on the basis of pregnancy, childbirth, and related medical conditions.

[4] On limited efforts to apply disparate impact to tenure discrimination cases, see the articles by Cooper (1983), West (1994), and Mahony (1987). Attempts to apply disparate impact in tenure discrimination cases based on sex (or race) include *Davis v. Weidner*, 596 F.2d 726 (7th Cir. 1979); *Campbell v. Ramsay*, 631 F.2d 597 (8th Cir. 1980); and *Scott v. University of Delaware*, 455 F. Supp. 1102 (D. Del. 1978).

Once the plaintiff has established a prima facie case, the burden shifts to the employer who must articulate a legitimate, nondiscriminatory reason for its decision. When the employer has met this burden, under *McDonnell Douglas* the plaintiff must prove that the employer's legitimate nondiscriminatory reason is not the real reason for the decision but rather a cover story or a "pretext" for discrimination.

During the past two decades, judicial interpretations have, for the most part, made it more difficult for a plaintiff in a tenure case to prove discrimination. Specifically, judicial interpretations of the question of "intent" to discriminate and the relative importance of motive have made it harder to prove sex discrimination. A major shift occurred when the Supreme Court ruled in *Texas Department of Community Affairs v. Burdine*, 450 U.S. 248 (1981), that the defendant must produce a legitimate, nondiscriminatory explanation for its decision but that the defendant does not have to persuade the court that it was actually motivated by this reason. For example, in tenure cases, universities typically explain that they denied tenure because of inadequate scholarship or teaching. Under *Burdine*, the college or university does not need to prove that it actually based its decision on this rationale, only that a decision based on this rationale would be reasonable. Thus, winning sex discrimination cases became more difficult after *Burdine*, because the burden of persuasion now remains with the plaintiff throughout the life of the case.

> **Judicial interpretations have, for the most part, made it more difficult for a plaintiff in a tenure case to prove discrimination.**

More recent Supreme Court rulings have imposed additional burdens on plaintiffs, most notably in *St. Mary's Honor Center v. Hicks*, 509 U.S. 502 (1993). In an opinion written by Justice Antonin Scalia, the Supreme Court concluded that even if a plaintiff could demonstrate that the employer lied about its reason for its employment decision, the plaintiff would also need to show that the employer lied specifically to mask discrimination. The pretext, Scalia reasoned, may simply be disguising a nondiscriminatory but unsavory reason such as personal dislike for the plaintiff, and in such cases, Title VII does not provide a remedy.

The U.S. Court of Appeals applied the *Hicks* decision to academia in the often-cited and important ruling *Fisher v. Vassar College*, 114 F.3d 1332 (2d Cir. 1997), a case supported by the Legal Advocacy Fund and discussed in Chapter 4. The *Fisher* court concluded:

> Individual decision-makers may intentionally dissemble in order to hide a reason that is nondiscriminatory but unbecoming or small-minded, such as back-scratching, log-rolling, horse-trading, institutional politics, envy, nepotism, spite, or personal hostility . . . . The fact that the proffered reason was false does not necessarily mean that the true motive was the illegal one argued by the plaintiff. (*Fisher*, 1337)

Because tenure decisions involve multiple decision makers, a decision will be made for multiple reasons. In a complex decision-making process, it becomes increasingly difficult for plaintiffs to demonstrate that the driving force behind the negative decision was discrimination.

More complicated Title VII disparate treatment cases involve "mixed motives" (both legitimate and discriminatory motives) for the employment decision. The Supreme Court addressed the issue of mixed motives in its landmark ruling in *Price Waterhouse v. Hopkins*, 490 U.S. 228 (1989), holding that *Price Waterhouse* had both legitimate and discriminatory reasons for denying partnership to the plaintiff. In affirming part of the lower court's ruling for Hopkins, Justice William Brennan determined that under Title VII, "the critical inquiry . . . is whether gender was a factor in the employment decision *at the moment it was made*" (*Price Waterhouse*, 241) [n.b., emphasis in the original opinion]. In other words, sex discrimination must have played a motivating part in the employment decision, but it need not be the only motivation.

The Civil Rights Act of 1991, which amended Title VII, codified the motivating factor standard.[5] Thus a plaintiff who can show that a decision was the product of a combination of legitimate and illegitimate motives has put forward direct evidence of discrimination and

> **Pinpointing sex discrimination amidst the tangled web of subjective judgments behind a tenure decision is a Herculean task.**

does not need to demonstrate pretext as required under the McDonnell Douglas paradigm. Under *Price Waterhouse*, "The plaintiff must persuade the factfinder on one point, and then the employer, if it wishes to prevail, must persuade it on another" (ibid., 246).

As the cases described herein illustrate, pinpointing sex discrimination amidst the tangled web of subjective judgments behind a tenure decision is a Herculean task. University decision makers are also becoming more adept at protecting the university from liability through a variety of means and by saying the right thing, if not actually doing the right thing.

Methodology

This report is based on an examination of 19 sex discrimination cases supported by the AAUW Legal Advocacy Fund. The research draws on a variety of public documents, as well as interviews with plaintiffs. The cases are described primarily from the plaintiffs' perspectives, but the defenses articulated by universities and colleges are also presented. No attempt is made to second-guess the courts' decisions. Rather, the report aims to address broader questions about sex discrimination in the academic workplace. What can we learn from these cases about sex discrimination in the academic setting? What can universities learn about their systems and practices of hiring and promotion? And what is the message for policy-makers considering new programs to end sex discrimination in academia and other professional settings?

---

[5] The Civil Rights Act of 1991 also codified an affirmative defense for employers during the remedy phase, limiting the available relief in mixed-motive cases.

Chapter Overview

Chapter 1 introduced the issue of sex discrimination in the academic tenure process. The remaining chapters are organized according to the phases of a typical sex discrimination case.

Chapter 2 discusses plaintiffs' allegations and the process of making a prima facie case of sex discrimination. Various types of sex discrimination claims that have been brought against universities are discussed. Allegations range from disparate treatment of female and male scholars to discounting women's studies to charges of a "chilly climate" that hinder women faculty.

Chapter 3 presents common strategies and arguments used by universities to counter plaintiffs' claims. Universities typically invoke one or both of the following arguments: academic freedom and the exceptional nature of the tenure decision. The chapter describes strategies such as delaying tactics, withholding of evidence, and settlement.

Chapter 4 delineates the ways in which a plaintiff demonstrates that the university's decision is based on pretext and this pretext covers up discriminatory intent. The chapter also examines the issue of direct evidence in mixed-motive cases, exploring what it takes for a plaintiff to prevail.

Chapter 5 describes the costs and rewards of pursuing sex discrimination lawsuits. In a sex discrimination lawsuit, plaintiffs may be awarded compensatory damages, back and front pay, or even reinstatement and tenure, as well as attorney's fees and costs. In practice, few plaintiffs are reinstated, and most compensation packages do not financially justify the enormous time and expense of the lawsuit. Yet many plaintiffs do find rewards in the process, largely from the satisfaction of fighting for what they believe is right.

Chapter 6 offers recommendations for universities and faculty to prevent sex discrimination and sex discrimination suits. Good employment policies, consistently applied, can go a long way toward preventing lawsuits. While women may not be able to avoid sex discrimination, we suggest strategies for dealing with discrimination that may help avoid the financial and other costs of litigation. The chapter concludes with advice for faculty who believe that they have been victims of sex discrimination and are considering legal action.

CHAPTER 2

Allegations: The Prima Facie Case of Discrimination

When a faculty member becomes a plaintiff in a sex discrimination case, she and her legal counsel must shape her experiences into a prima facie legal case. That is, the plaintiff must demonstrate that she has enough evidence for her case to be heard by a court. The plaintiff can do this in several ways. She can attempt to show procedural irregularities, such as a failure to collect all available evidence on her candidacy, or she can present conventional evidence of bias on the part of individuals involved in her decision. She can show that she was denied tenure despite support from a significant percentage of departmental faculty or other scholars in her field. Some courts have admitted statistical data concerning the percentage of tenured female faculty as sufficient to make a prima facie case, and others will consider a "hostile environment" in the department (Cooper 1983).

This chapter examines allegations of sex discrimination from cases supported by the AAUW Legal Advocacy Fund. Some plaintiffs' stories match the popular stereotypes of discrimination, describing a relationship with a tormenting and belittling nemesis who plays a critical role in the plaintiff's professional life. Other plaintiffs alleged that they had experienced sexual harassment or retaliation for acting as whistle-blowers against male faculty accused of harassment.

This chapter also describes subtler forms of sex discrimination, such as the failure to consistently apply policies regarding pregnancy and childbirth or the allegation that publications in women's studies are not counted fairly in the tenure decision. These kinds of discrimination may be less obvious than the archaic assertion that a professor is too feminine, as described in the flagship case *Zahorik v. Cornell University*, 579 F. Supp. 349 (N.D.N.Y. 1983), or the equally inappropriate assertion that a female professor is too aggressive and does not conform to her colleagues' ideas of how women should behave, as alleged in Carol Stepien's case against Case Western Reserve University, described later in this chapter. These "second generation" cases deserve special attention as the new frontier in sex discrimination law, not only in academia but in other workplaces as well.

Departures From Procedural Norms

When a department or university violates its own procedures or customary practices in a tenure review, the rejected candidate—and the court—inevitably wonders why. Because tenure decisions involve several different levels of decision makers and committees, ample opportunity exists for both honest error and impermissible manipulation of the process for discriminatory ends. A lack of integrity or consistency in the tenure process—for example, the distortion and rejection of positive outside references, the suppression of favorable reviews, or the improper solicitation of external peer reviews—does not by itself prove that a female professor has been denied tenure for illegitimate reasons such as sex discrimination. It does invite speculation along those lines, however, and in the legal arena ultimately may be sufficient to support an inference of discrimination.

> When a department or university violates its own procedures or customary practices in a tenure review, the rejected candidate—and the court—inevitably wonders why.

***

Marcia Falk, a widely published poet, translator, and feminist critic, joined the University of Judaism Department of English in 1984 as an associate professor of literature. She applied for tenure in late 1985. From the outset, procedural questions delayed and complicated Falk's tenure bid, with the evaluating committee and Falk wrangling about the quantity and organization of materials for her tenure dossier. The committee insisted on anonymity, so Falk had no opportunity to discuss the process with committee members. The university's published procedures for tenure and promotion did not require an anonymous review committee, thus the secrecy around Falk's tenure review was the first of many departures from normal procedure.

Access to information about the evaluation process was an issue throughout Falk's tenure review. The committee refused to let Falk review outside letters of reference, allowing her to see only a summary report purportedly synthesizing the letters. Pursuant to a request by Falk, investigators from the American Association of University Professors read the original letters and the summary and concluded, "One has difficulty recognizing that the letters and the report are discussing the same publications and the same person" (AAUP 1988, 27). For example, the evaluating committee summarized that one reviewer "repeatedly evinces hesitations about the frequent failure of [Falk's] poems to engage." The reviewer's actual letter, while not without qualification, was decidedly more positive:

> Her syntax is simple and her language almost ascetically modest. . . . This mode can shade off into the commonplace. For the most part, however, she writes a taut, precise plain style that proves that she is unafraid to be straightforward yet alert to nuance. . . . [Her poems] testify to a lucid intelligence and a solid craftsmanship. She is a poet who will bear watching. . . . I recommend warmly for promotion to full professor. (Ibid.)

In a final procedural anomaly, the university provided no mechanism for Falk to receive a response to her allegations of sex discrimination in the tenure process. The AAUP report concluded, "The possibility is distinct, although it cannot be determined with certainty, that discrimination based on sex . . . contributed significantly" to the university's rejection of Falk's candidacy (ibid., 28).

Falk argued that sex discrimination was behind the departures from the normal tenure review process, and the AAUP investigation noted that some administrators expressed a personal dislike for Falk that may have been based on her sex and on her work as a feminist critic teaching in a conservative Jewish university. The university emphatically denied this hypothesis, arguing that other professors also engaged in critical, iconoclastic scholarship.

An investigation by the U.S. Equal Employment Opportunity Commission also identified procedural irregularities in the handling of Falk's tenure application and found reasonable cause to believe that Falk's charge of sex discrimination in the denial of tenure was true. Falk filed a lawsuit in 1988 and settled her case against the University of Judaism in 1991.

Although Falk no longer has a full-time academic appointment, she continues to teach and publish. In 2001 she was the Priesand Visiting Professor of Jewish Women's Studies at Hebrew Union College in Cincinnati.

***

Professor of art history Margaretta Lovell wrestled with similar procedural issues during her tenure review process at the University of California, Berkeley. When she appealed her two negative tenure reviews to the university's privilege and tenure committee, the committee "made an unprecedented recommendation to the Chancellor that [Lovell] 'be given tenure without further review. . . . A favorable tenure decision would have been forthcoming earlier, as a result of the regular review process, had it not been for irregularities throughout [Lovell's] case'" (Lovell, Testimony, 1990, 5).

The university's own oversight committee found that the art history department seemed to have given "no weight to substantial achievements in the usual categories" for tenure review and ignored

Lovell's standing in the national and international community of art historians (ibid., 3). The committee identified several factual errors as well, including, as in the Falk case, a "scornful" department report that subverted and overlooked positive aspects of Lovell's dossier in violation of the policy that departmental reviews be "fair" to the candidate and appraise all favorable and unfavorable evidence (ibid., 4). The university's Title IX officer characterized this department report as so at odds with the department's procedures and "so rife with hostility that I have no trouble dismissing it altogether" (ibid., 5).

In her 1990 court complaint, Lovell charged that the university violated established rules in her tenure review. She alleged that the university allowed biased members of the art history department to insert erroneous and prejudicial documents into her personnel files; refused to provide her with access to confidential materials in her file or summarize their contents; refused to provide a statement of the reason for her tenure denial; assessed her based on an incomplete record; and forced her to undergo a second departmental deliberation that used irregular voting procedures, failed to consider information favorable to the plaintiff, actively misrepresented favorable information, and knowingly reinserted errors into the file.

While disturbing procedural errors do not constitute sex discrimination in and of themselves, Lovell suspected gender bias because between her positive reviews in 1986 and her notably less positive reviews in 1988, she had advocated better treatment of female graduate students and faculty. In particular, she had publicly objected to the disproportionate assignment of service responsibilities to women faculty. The Title IX officer for the university found that irregularities in the process, coupled with Lovell's advocacy for women, pointed to clear discrimination based on sex. The officer's report concluded that the department's assessment of Lovell "violated the Faculty Code of Conduct . . . which identifies as 'unacceptable conduct: Making evaluations of the professional competence of faculty members by criteria not directly reflective of professional performance'" (ibid., 5).

Lovell settled her case in 1992. She is now a full professor with tenure at the university.

Tenure Denial From Above

During the last decade, administrators have increasingly reversed positive departmental tenure recommendations. Elite universities such as Yale, Stanford, and Harvard have had relatively high-profile cases in which female candidates have been supported enthusiastically at the departmental level and then been rejected by deans, provosts, or presidents. Harvard's president, for example, denied tenure to political theorist Bonnie Honig in 1997 despite strong departmental support and Honig's status, according to many, as a star in her field.

A vocal minority in the department who oppose tenure can, in effect, lobby behind the scenes to have a positive recommendation reversed.

A panel of deans at Stanford University rejected a unanimously positive departmental vote for historian Karen Sawislak in 1997, and a committee of deans at Yale similarly denied tenure to Diane Kunz, who enjoyed strong departmental support. As Kunz noted, "The bastions are not falling" for women seeking tenure at the most prestigious schools" (Wilson 1997).

Because tenure should be based on the quality of a candidate's scholarship, teaching, and service—all of which are arguably most accurately appraised by other faculty—some faculty view the intervention of administrators as inappropriate (Wilson 1997; Magner 1997). Female faculty members are particularly concerned, for a variety of reasons. When administrators have substantive roles in the tenure review process, a vocal minority in the department who oppose tenure can, in effect, lobby behind the scenes to have a positive recommendation reversed.

Harvard University Law School professor Clare Dalton settled a sex discrimination suit with the law school when it denied her tenure and believes backdoor lobbying and negotiations affected the decision. She speculated, "There may be people in the minority who have access to folks higher up in the process" (Wilson 1997). Given that women are underrepresented as administrators and senior faculty, male professors are more likely to enjoy long-established, informal collegiality with deans than are female professors, who are fewer in number.

Some observers argue that administrators must intervene in the tenure process because departments are recommending tenure for too many candidates. A Stanford University dean claimed, "Administrators have had to intervene to make the difficult decisions that the departments won't make themselves." According to the dean, departments vote to grant tenure in the majority of cases, which, he believes, is simply untenable for a prestigious university that should maintain exceedingly high standards (ibid.). Nonetheless, when administrators step in to make the hard decision, they risk opening the door to a sex discrimination lawsuit.

***

Art professor Catherine Clinger breezed through the first stages of the tenure process at New Mexico Highlands University. She had been unanimously approved by her department, the dean, and the vice president of academic affairs. "Where I got 'dissed' was at the regents level," she claimed. The regents' vote was typically a pro forma one, as it is in most universities, where the board rubber-stamps tenure recommendations from the department and academic officers. When Clinger attended the university board meeting, she had the humiliating experience of hearing that she would not get tenure after all. "It was the last order of business," she recalled. "Everyone was there for a celebration. Then they took a head-to-head vote on each of the candidates and later promotion, and right there . . . I heard them say no."

The university argued that it denied Clinger tenure because she did not have a terminal degree in printmaking, which is not unusual in some professional fields. Clinger countered that this was clearly a pretext, given that a male candidate had received tenure with fewer qualifications and the university had granted tenure to faculty with-out relevant terminal degrees in their disciplines. Furthermore, the university advertisement for Clinger's position stated that the candidate should possess *either* a terminal degree *or* "equivalent experience and professional record in printmaking." Clinger had more than 16 years of professional experience as well as a master's degree in art history and had earned the status of master printer, deemed superior to a master's degree in her field. Finally, Clinger had earned the support of her peers in the department and among the academic officers at the university (AAUP 1999).

AAUP investigators agreed with Clinger's claims of bias. While the university's steadfast insistence on a terminal master's degree was "facially legitimate," the investigators noted, the board had "acted against the judgment of all the academic recommending bodies at the university," and Clinger was afforded no opportunity for institutional review of her allegations (ibid.).

Clinger was optimistic until she had her first meeting with the university about the case. "Talk about disillusionment," she recalled. Clinger thought the university would offer a settlement and she would have to decide whether she wanted to be reinstated or not. "I was willing to stay and be tortured" at the school, she wryly noted. "I wanted my job back." The university made Clinger a meager settlement offer of $5,000, which she rejected. The court granted the university's motion for dismissal on summary judgment in 1999, and Clinger's appeals did not succeed.

Clinger's attorneys believed that the First Amendment issues (Clinger's right to publicly criticize the regents) pending in her case merited an appeal to the U.S. Supreme Court, but Clinger—while moving forward on other claims—did not pursue the sex discrimination charge, which was more difficult to develop. The Supreme Court did not hear the case, so Clinger's litigation ended in 2001.

Clinger has returned to school to earn a doctorate in art history at University College London.

Comparisons to Similarly Situated Male Colleagues

A professor applying for tenure is evaluated in comparison to peers at her university and peers in her specialty at other universities. These comparisons are at the core of many sex discrimination cases. In such cases, a plaintiff needs to find a "similarly situated" male colleague to serve as a point of comparison. Plaintiffs can demonstrate discrimination, at least in part, by showing that male candidates with similar or inferior qualifications in teaching, scholarship, or service received promotions, higher pay, or tenure while female candidates did not.

A similarly situated man is hard to find. A plaintiff who builds a case around a comparison with a tenured male colleague must show that the colleague had comparable or inferior qualifications and that the plaintiff and her colleague were considered for tenure in roughly the same time period. Universities typically consider only a few candidates for tenure each year, however, and these candidates are likely to teach in different departments and disciplines with different criteria and measures of success. Candidates in highly specialized areas often have few or no comparable colleagues undergoing the tenure process at the same time. Because tenure standards have escalated during the past several decades, the records of colleagues who received tenure under the less rigorous standards of earlier generations cannot be used for comparison.

A similarly situated man is hard to find.

On paper, making a comparison to a similarly situated male colleague seems straightforward—it is a matter of counting publications, classes taught, and service activities. In practice, however, these comparisons are rarely straightforward. For example, publications can be evaluated differently because the relative quality of journals, book publishers, and other accomplishments is often a matter of debate. A tenure file is somewhat like a Rorschach test, saying as much about the reviewer as the applicant.

***

Lucinda Miller, a former professor of pharmacy practice, sued Texas Tech University Health Sciences Center for sex discrimination in the denial of tenure (as well as pay inequity in violation of the Equal Pay Act). Miller also alleged that the school retaliated when she complained about the discrimination.

In 1997 the Texas Tech School of Pharmacy hired Miller as a professor and vice chair of the pharmacy practice department. The school also hired a female, who would later become Miller's co-plaintiff, as an associate dean. According to Miller, the university assured the new hires that they would be considered for tenure immediately. During the hiring process, Miller was told that that the institution was prohibited from paying her more than a specified base salary and $5,000 as an administrative stipend, although she later discovered that other professors were paid more.

While at Texas Tech, Miller carried a full teaching load, published several scholarly articles, was the founding editor of a new scholarly journal, and established a clinical program for the School of Pharmacy. She also served on eight committees and chaired five of them. In 1998 Miller and her female colleague submitted tenure applications. Each had written numerous publications and received prestigious recognition. At that time, only one other professor, a male applicant, was eligible for tenure. Despite favorable recommendations and praise from outside reviewers, Miller and her female colleague were both denied tenure, and the male applicant was awarded tenure.

Both women felt that they had been unfairly denied tenure. Miller compared her 63 publications in peer-reviewed journals and 84 publications overall to her male colleague's three peer-reviewed publications and 16 publications overall. Miller elaborated that her male colleague's scholarly record was even weaker than these numbers suggest because the bulk of his non-peer-reviewed publications appeared in his monthly column in *Drug Topics*, which was not considered an academic journal. Miller, in contrast, had published in top-tier medical journals such as the *Archives of Internal Medicine* and the *American Journal of Psychiatry*, which were considered far more prestigious forums, and was primary author of 61 of her 63 publications. Additionally, she had published a book, founded a journal, and had a copyright and one patent; her male colleague had none of these accomplishments. In the critical area of research funding and grants, Miller had secured almost a half million dollars in research money.

In response to her EEOC complaint, the university alleged that Miller had applied for tenure prematurely. The university denied assuring Miller that she would be considered for tenure immediately and rejected her tenure application because she had not completed sufficient teaching, clinical practice, or research at Texas Tech. The chair questioned Miller's excellence in teaching and research and asserted that Miller had not attained a national reputation in the field.

Miller and her female colleague alleged that they were subjected to a hostile environment and that procedural irregularities occurred throughout the tenure process. The chair of the tenure committee allegedly informed faculty affairs committee members that the male applicant's tenure application would receive a "smooth highway" but the women's tenure applications would not (*Miller v. Texas Tech*, Complaint, 2000, 7). The work environment was so unbearable for Miller that she resigned in March 1999.

Miller and her colleague filed a joint lawsuit in U.S. District Court in 2000. Faculty and former students came to the aid of Miller and her female co-plaintiff with affidavits and depositions, and the two assembled nearly a dozen individuals to serve as expert witnesses. The university subsequently filed a motion for summary judgment that was denied. The university filed additional motions with the 5th U.S. Circuit Court of Appeals regarding disability claims of Miller's co-plaintiff, which has delayed trial.

Miller continues to await her day in court.

***

Biology professor Ricky Hirschhorn's case against the University of Kentucky presents a similar illustration of differential standards and comparisons. When she was denied tenure by the University of Kentucky in 1990, Hirschhorn questioned the criteria by which she had failed to measure up to her male colleagues. The department chair had described the school's expectations for scholarly productivity as about one peer-reviewed journal article per year. Hirschhorn reviewed the publication records of senior faculty in her department and discovered that the five senior faculty members had averaged less than one publication a year and that her record, with one paper in preparation, would easily equal this average. She also found that her articles had been cited in high-impact journals within her specialty, another gauge of high-quality, important scholarly work. She then asked the chancellor whether perhaps a lack of success in getting extramural funding impeded her tenure chances. Here, too, Hirschhorn had accomplished more than many of her colleagues: Half of the faculty in her department had not brought in these funds or applied for grants in the past four years.

Finally, Hirschhorn expressed bewilderment over the tenure decision given her earlier positive reviews. In the late 1980s her performance evaluations suggested a positive momentum toward tenure and excellent progress in her research program. By 1990, when her performance evaluation expressed concern about her publication record, Hirschhorn was left to speculate that the criteria must have been dramatically altered.

Hirschhorn was not passive about the tenure process. She asked three different directors for a description of the department's expectations for a positive tenure review but was never given an answer. She hypothesized that expectations must have changed from one director to another, recasting what one director had described as a strong research record to a marginal one. Her department had never established criteria for tenure and promotion, thereby denying her firm criteria to assess her progress.

Hirschhorn lost her case at trial in 1995, and her appeal was denied. In part, Hirschhorn lost because she failed to find a similarly situated man, a required element of her prima facie case. Her investigations led her to draw comparisons to senior faculty, but such comparisons were not compelling to the court because senior faculty are not, strictly speaking, similarly situated to junior faculty seeking tenure.

Hirschhorn is now an associate professor of biology and director of the Graduate Biomedical Science Program at Hood College in Maryland.

Pregnancy Discrimination

An academic career can be surprisingly unfriendly to pregnant women and mothers, in large part because the tenure clock often collides with the biological clock. The typical graduate student attends graduate school for more than seven years and is 33 years old when she or he graduates with a doctorate and enters the job market (Hoffer et al. 2003, 23). This long training period poses a dilemma for aspiring women faculty.

Younger female faculty hear stories of trailblazing women who sacrificed children and family for their profession, and a rich lode of anecdote and lore among female academicians suggests the optimal and worst times to give birth. Some academics urge female professors to play biological roulette and postpone childbearing until after tenure. Others advise women to try to have children before applying for tenure-track jobs, perhaps initially after completion of the dissertation. Still others share stories of promising candidates who were, they allege, denied tenure because of the "distraction" of babies and child care.

The tenure clock often collides with the biological clock.

Pregnancy and motherhood affect women's promotion in academe in direct and indirect ways, and anecdotal evidence suggests that this form of sex discrimination should be monitored more closely. Not only are most women mothers at some point in their lives, but all women of childbearing age can be viewed as potential mothers. Few colleges or universities openly admit to harboring discriminatory intent, and, indeed, as women become more commonplace in academe, they more easily enjoy genuine respect and collegiality from their male peers. A more subtle form of discrimination persists, however, regarding mothers' commitment to serious scholarship. Unspoken assumptions about women and motherhood can cloud the judgment of even well-meaning colleagues.

***

When political science professor Jill Crystal was denied tenure by the University of Michigan, she alleged pregnancy discrimination and retaliation for demanding her right under the Pregnancy Discrimination Act of 1978 (an amendment to Title VII). Her accusation was multifold. In a report to the grievance review board, Crystal detailed numerous "serious, willful, and multiple violations of procedures and norms at the Department level" that "contaminated" her tenure review (1993, 107). She further contended that her tenure denial was part of a general pattern of sex discrimination, which was manifested in a "thread of secrecy and deceit" in the department's tenure reviews for three female candidates, including herself (ibid., 131). Crystal charged that the university essentially held women to a different standard if they were not permitted time off following childbirth.

After she announced her pregnancy in 1990, Crystal discovered that the university did not have a written maternity policy. In practice, the university typically required pregnant women to take off a semester without pay. The de facto policy encouraged women to give birth either during their research leave or during the summer. Thus their absences affected their research, on which their promotions most heavily depended, rather than their teaching.

Without paid leave, Crystal noted, "the burden fell on the women to solve what the University defined as [the women's] problem" (ibid., 145). Crystal realized that this was a violation of the Pregnancy Discrimination Act and pursued the matter with the administration. After months of negotiations and discussions, the university offered to allow her to take the fall term off at full pay, an arrangement in conformity with the law and satisfactory to Crystal. Yet Crystal concluded, "I won the battle, but I lost the war" (ibid., 148). Crystal believed that because she had exercised her right to maternity leave, the university branded her a troublemaker and, at the first opportunity, fired her.

Crystal's discussions with other female faculty provide a ground-level view of the direct and indirect obstacles to tenure for mothers. Professors described to Crystal that they made heroic efforts to return to teaching immediately after childbirth ("I . . . came back in 2.5 weeks"), tried to plan pregnancies for the summer ("My . . . chair mentioned something to me about summer being the best time to have a kid"), relied on the personal generosity and flexibility of their departmental colleagues and chairs ("Thanks to the support of my chairperson . . . things worked well for me"), or improvised other solutions (ibid., 143). They found, in one woman's terms, "informal and individual ways of maneuvering around" the university's policies (ibid., 144). According to Crystal, several female professors believed that pregnancy had hampered their chances for tenure because they were viewed as less serious about or committed to their careers, limiting their productive research time and service contributions or creating animosity concerning teaching responsibilities.

Crystal filed a lawsuit against the University of Michigan in 1993. A court-ordered mediation panel found in her favor in 1996, and she was awarded $100,000.

Crystal now teaches at Auburn University.

***

In another discrimination case involving pregnancy and motherhood, Sonia Goltz sued the University of Notre Dame, alleging that because she was not given time off following childbirth, she was held to a higher standard (because she had less time to prepare her tenure dossier). Notre Dame did have a "stop-the-tenure-clock" rule but, according to Goltz, it was not applied fairly. As described later in this chapter, she also argued that she was subjected to a hostile work environment.

Recognizing the time-consuming nature of infant care, some universities have adopted a policy of allowing new parents, predominantly women, to wait an additional year before tenure review. Because she was not permitted this additional year, Goltz charged that Notre Dame held her to a different standard for tenure than it held her male peers. Notre Dame's unwillingness to stop the tenure clock in Goltz's case made her record appear weaker vis-à-vis male colleagues and vis-à-vis female colleagues who had become faculty earlier than she but had given birth to children after Notre Dame implemented a new maternity leave policy. When Notre Dame implemented the policy, they made it retroactive to include faculty who had given birth up to two years preceding its formulation. Goltz missed this window and was not grandfathered into the provision.

Goltz's colleague Beth Kern was given an extra year on the tenure clock but was not told that the university expected an extra year's worth of publications, an expectation that runs counter to the spirit of the policy. Both women alleged that they were held to the wrong standard. In their joint 1993 narrative to the EEOC, Goltz and Kern, who worked in the College of Business, noted that even before Notre Dame formulated its tenure-clock maternity policy, the College of Sciences had regularly given its assistant professors an additional year on the tenure clock for a variety of reasons. They cited a faculty member who was given an extra year for medical reasons as an example. "The university seems to have no problem granting this additional time," Goltz and Kern wrote, "but is reluctant to grant additional time for those who have children" (1993, 18).

Goltz and other female faculty in the College of Business hesitated even to take the four-week disability leave immediately following birth, sensing "pressure in the College of Business not to take it. . . . Taking a four week maternity leave may be seen by some members of the committee as a lack of commitment to career, and a premeditated plan to cause an imposition" (ibid., 23).

Goltz and Kern documented several incidents, from ephemeral remarks to policies that communicated departmental hostility toward child-rearing. Echoing Jill Crystal's account of her experiences at the University of Michigan—and the informal expectation at many schools—Notre Dame's president commented during discussions of the maternity leave policy that perhaps women could time their births to occur during breaks in the academic year. "This is an interesting comment for a Catholic priest to make," Goltz and Kern wryly observed, and a rather unrealistic expectation given the lack of predictability of conception, especially for older women.

Goltz returned to the classroom five days after she gave birth, "fearing that her department would hold it against her if she took a few weeks' leave." She noted that announcement of her child's birth, which was posted in the faculty mail room, was torn down several times (ibid., 24).

Faculty and the administration seemed to maintain a children-or-career antinomy for female professors. An associate dean said to another professor, "Perhaps you can be like Sonia [Goltz] and not take any time off" after a pregnancy (ibid.). Kern was approached by "several faculty members after tenure denial with a statement to the effect of now you'll have to decide what you're going to do—meaning full-time motherhood or continuing as a professor" (ibid., 25).

Hostile Work Environments

A hostile work environment is characterized by sexist jokes, banter, exclusion from social events, and other behavior that makes employees feel uncomfortable and unwanted. In a chilly work environment, coauthorship and other forms of collaboration among senior and junior faculty are unlikely, which can weaken a candidate's case for tenure. This environment can also be accompanied by differences in the kinds of work assigned to men and women.

***

According to Sonia Goltz and Beth Kern, the University of Notre Dame College of Business was a hostile work environment. Incidents included inappropriate sexual banter and exclusion from social activities. For example, the accounting department celebrated a male colleague's birthday with a "boob cake" in the shape of a woman's breast (Fosmoe 1998). When an employee turned down dates with male faculty members, male faculty openly bantered that she "must be a lesbian" (Goltz & Kern 1993, 22). A couple of women signed up for an athletic team only to discover the next day that a new sheet had appeared in the faculty mail room stating, "Any new person, poor player, and all women can sign up for a second team. . . . The primary team would consist of the people who had been playing together prior to the women requesting membership" (ibid., 10). Discrimination against women faculty could also be seen in the assignment of teaching responsibilities. Goltz was not assigned to teach graduate courses. Since the college was hoping to establish a doctoral program, this lack of experience with graduate students made her less attractive for promotion to tenure. For Kern, the problem was an unusually heavy teaching load, limiting the time available for research and publications.

Service loads differed as well, and women were "asked to perform service significantly more often" than men were (ibid., 14). Service, while nominally a criterion for tenure, in fact receives scant attention in the evaluation process. Goltz and Kern attributed Notre Dame's increased demands on women for service to the "appearance of a crowd" ploy, where schools ask women faculty—as well as faculty of color—to attend more functions and serve on more committees than their white, male counterparts so that the school could appear to have adequate representation by underrepresented groups. Since women comprised less than 10 percent of Notre Dame's College of Business faculty, Kern and Goltz were asked to appear at many functions "to present an image of having a substantial number of women on the faculty" (ibid., 15). By the same logic, they were asked to meet with prospective female faculty in other departments, a simple task that could, in fact, consume many hours and had almost no value in a tenure review (ibid., 16).

In and of itself, any one of these instances would not necessarily constitute sex discrimination. But when an incident becomes part of a pattern of exclusion and when this exclusion has professional ramifications, it constitutes sex discrimination. For Kern and Goltz, the sexist climate and uneven treatment of men and women led ultimately to negative tenure reviews and grueling lawsuits.

Goltz lost her case at trial in 1998. She is now an associate professor of management at Michigan Technological University. Kern settled her case in 1998 and now directs the master of science and accounting program at Indiana University, Southbend.

Bias Against Women's Studies

As women have entered academia in growing numbers, many are challenging established curricula in fundamental ways. Since the 1970s, women's studies programs and scholarly journals have proliferated. Some academics appear to be biased against women's studies, however, discounting publications in women's studies journals in their assessment of scholarly productivity. While students have embraced classes in women's studies—and articles on gender have been published in many well-respected scholarly journals—some academics remain skeptical, albeit usually silently.

Women's studies scholars face difficulties in tenure reviews because their work cuts across disciplines and is published in women's studies journals rather than the journals the department considers to be top-tier. A women's studies scholar based in a history department, for example, may have published her most significant work in a top-tier interdisciplinary journal such as *Signs* or *Feminist Studies* but not in a top-tier history journal such as the *American Historical Review*. This means that colleagues not disposed to women's studies may feel that her scholarship is inadequate for tenure. In *Lynn v. Regents of the University of California*, 656 F.2d 1337, 1343 (9th Cir. 1981), the court found, "A disdain for women's issues, and a diminished opinion of those who concentrate on those issues, is evidence of a discriminatory attitude towards women." Plaintiffs supported by LAF have made similar allegations.

> *A disdain for women's issues, and a diminished opinion of those who concentrate on those issues, is evidence of a discriminatory attitude towards women.*

***

Among other allegations, Diana Paul, an Asian American professor of religion who filed a sex and race discrimination case against Stanford University and whose case is also discussed in Chapter 3, argued that her colleagues belittled feminist scholarship. The summary of the personnel committee's report on Paul to the dean included disparaging remarks about feminist studies. The department noted that Paul's conclusion in one piece consisted of "feminist ideological declarations" and saw her material on feminism as "appropriate and timely . . . but . . . it does not evidence long-range promise of scholarly distinction." Paul noted that her department's attitude toward feminist studies contrasted with the stated position of Stanford in the faculty handbook, which declared, "The study of race and gender in history . . . has moved from the periphery of attention to an important role in understanding the development of society" (*Paul v. Stanford*, Declaration, January 6, 1986, 40).

Paul recalled that when she applied for tenure, the chair of her department told her that he had recommended against tenure for a professor in the history department because her work focused too heavily on women. The only tenure-track woman in the department competent to teach feminist issues, Paul also shouldered substantial service burdens and extracurricular demands. She chaired a curriculum review panel, the M.A. in Feminist Studies Committee, and the East Asian Studies Committee and served as a member of the Feminist Studies Committee, in addition to other service responsibilities (ibid., 39). Paul argued, "The Department not only did not consider my attention to feminist studies an asset, they belittled the field and behaved with hostility towards it" (ibid., 40).

The judge in Paul's case found persuasive evidence that Paul would be able to establish a prima facie case based on the belittling of women's studies, women in general, and Japanese women in particular by senior faculty in decision-making positions. The former chair of the department, the judge concluded, "demonstrated on numerous occasions that he thought of Asian women as playthings, unworthy of professional dignities afforded professors" (*Paul v. Stanford University*, 1986 WL 614, 6 [1986]).

Paul settled her case in 1986 and received $54,000.

Collegiality

Courts have recognized collegiality, a candidate's working relationships with other faculty and students, as a valid, nondiscriminatory basis for tenure and promotion decisions. The concept has gained currency in sex discrimination cases since it was first recognized in higher education case law in 1981 in *Mayberry v. Dees*, 663 F.2d 502 (4th Cir. 1981). Among the standards for tenure, the collegiality criterion is the most easily abused. Lack of collegiality can be applied to any candidate whose demeanor, personality, academic interests, or political beliefs clash with those of senior faculty members.

The American Association of University Professors recently cautioned that the collegiality criterion lets in through the back door what Title VII shuts out at the front door, namely, a legally valid rationale for denying tenure to colleagues with unpopular feminist beliefs or those whose gender makes their colleagues uncomfortable. According to Martin Snyder of AAUP, recent collegiality cases "all came down to the same thing. They're all-male dominated departments that hadn't tenured a woman in a long time, or ever, and there's some language about how the woman 'just doesn't fit in.' What comes through is the sense that these are aggressive women who are seen as uppity" (Lewin 2002).

> *Lack of collegiality can be applied to any candidate whose demeanor, personality, academic interests, or political beliefs clash with those of senior faculty members.*

Some women have filed suits contending that collegiality is a smoke screen for denying tenure to women. *Stein v. Kent State University Board of Trustees*, 994 F. Supp. 898, 909 (N.D. Ohio 1998), summarized the prevailing legal interpretation: "The ability to get along with co-workers, when not a subterfuge for sex discrimination, is a legitimate consideration for tenure decisions." The trick is to distinguish the valid from the invalid applications of this ambiguous criterion.

Collegiality is so inextricably intertwined with personality and ideology that it can serve as a legally sanctioned wild card for discrimination. Colleagues may subconsciously penalize a female candidate because she is too feminine to fit their image of a colleague or, conversely, because her behavior seems too masculine. Gender-based stereotyping may be translated into assertions that a woman does not fit into the department and that she, therefore, lacks collegiality. While colleagues may perceive this gap as a personality clash, a plaintiff might just as accurately perceive it as job loss caused by her gender.

***

Carol Stepien opted to fight back when Case Western Reserve University's all-male tenured biology faculty denied her tenure. Her department did not dispute the quality of her training, scholarship, or research accomplishments because Stepien had been prolific and quite successful in publications and grants. In her view, she had been ensnared and impeded in her tenure bid by a department that had "all the characteristics of an old boys' club" (Mangels 2001). In this "chilly and hostile work environment," Stepien alleged, "it was extremely unlikely that I would be able to prepare for a successful tenure review" (Mangels 2000, 14).

The biology department introduced the theme of collegiality in 1994 in Stepien's annual review, citing two examples of poor interactions. The review described a weeklong class trip to the Bahamas that Stepien had organized and for which she had sought reimbursement for her overnight babysitting expenses of $315 for her 6-year-old son. Stepien had received conflicting information about whether or not the expenses were reimbursable, so she submitted the receipt. "Instead of simply telling me this wasn't an allowable expense," Stepien stated, the department chair "took it up with the senior faculty and then with the Dean's Office and the provost. . . . He presented it to others as if I was trying to deceive in some way" (ibid., 15). Her annual review cited the incident as evidence of a lack of collegiality.

According to Stepien, she received no explanation for her denial of tenure. Stepien appealed the decision to Case Western's grievance committees before filing an EEOC complaint and, eventually, a lawsuit in federal court in March 2001.

Stepien's critics felt that she could not get along with colleagues. Her supporters saw gender as central to the friction between Stepien and her department. "There might be a perception," speculated a former colleague of Stepien's at another school, "that, as a woman, [Stepien] should have a warm and fuzzy personality. She's not a warm and fuzzy person. Carol has a very strong personality. [But] it's inappropriate for people to make [tenure] decisions based on that" (ibid., 22).

Another former colleague, who served on both of Stepien's grievance panels, similarly argued that some faculty "don't realize that often they—men and women—expect women to make [faculty] feel comfortable, and . . . don't expect men to make [faculty] feel comfortable." When women don't make faculty feel comfortable, faculty "register that as being difficult" (ibid., 15). This discomfort around the female colleague can provoke her annoyance and anger, which in turn compounds the collegiality charge. A sympathetic colleague interpreted the collegiality charge to mean that Stepien "doesn't do what they want, because she doesn't step aside" (Smallwood 2001, A15).

Case Western's grievance panel concluded as much when they found that the department "may not be comfortable with Professor Stepien's style" and thus may have "inadvertently engaged in gender discrimination" (Mangels 2000, 17).

Stepien settled her lawsuit in May 2002. Today she is a tenured full professor of ecology and director of the Lake Erie Center at the University of Toledo.

Payback and Retaliation

Advocacy for women's rights in academia can be as risky as it is necessary. Informally, women are often counseled to wait until tenure before "rocking the boat." The five or six years before the tenure vote, however, can go by slowly for a woman working in a hostile work environment, and rocking the boat may

Advocacy and whistle-blowing can lead to serious consequences.

be necessary to put a stop to abusive treatment of oneself or others. Female advocates and whistler-blowers are rarely thanked by their colleagues, and advocacy and whistle-blowing can lead to serious consequences, such as the denial of tenure.

***

Voicing one's concerns about hostile or harassing behavior is a risky endeavor. In the case of Lynn Ilon, an economist in the State University of New York Buffalo Graduate School of Education, complaints of a male colleague's inappropriate behavior instigated a long battle of retaliation. Her complaint filed with the Niagara County, New York, Supreme Court in 2000 summarizes her case.

In 1994, Ilon contended that a male colleague sought her complicity in varying the final exam procedure for a female student. When Ilon refused to cooperate, the male colleague continued to pursue the matter, confronting her in such a way that she reported fearing for her physical safety. Throughout the next four years, according to Ilon, the male colleague remained hostile. She also alleged that he usurped her work. She felt that he treated her like a subordinate and that his attitude toward her stemmed from her gender. During this time, Ilon learned that the male colleague had made sexual advances to female students. She told senior colleagues about his alleged inappropriate behavior, but no action was taken. In December 1998, Ilon formally asked the university to investigate this colleague.

Ilon wanted to apply for tenure in February 1999 but withdrew her application when she realized that the male colleague would deliberate on her application. In March 1999 the university's equal opportunity and affirmative action office advised Ilon to suspend her complaint against her colleague to facilitate her tenure review. Ilon reapplied for tenure in 2000 but problems with her male colleague were raised during the tenure process, and the university president rejected Ilon's tenure application.

To Ilon, her colleague's behavior and her failed tenure bid were clearly related. She argued that she was denied tenure as retaliation by senior colleagues for her protests against the male colleague's behavior toward herself and students. She alleged that the university inadequately investigated her complaint and took no steps to remedy the situation. From early 1998 until her tenure denial, her adversary and his colleagues made decisions about Ilon's teaching schedule, advisers, and work rules without consulting her. In addition, Ilon alleged that the colleague and others engaged in a months-long smear campaign against her. They portrayed Ilon as "uncooperative and difficult to get along with," attempted to cast her performance in a negative light, and maneuvered her into the "awkward position of working with and supporting [the male colleague] or appearing uncooperative." Ilon's "refusal" to work with him, in turn, was marshaled by the university as evidence of her lack of commitment to the department (*Ilon v. SUNY Buffalo*, Complaint, November 27, 2000, 6).

In 2000, Ilon filed a lawsuit in state court alleging, in part, retaliation under state law. In 2004, the case is near the end of the discovery (fact-finding) phase of litigation.

***

Even after a faculty member has received tenure, she may encounter sex discrimination. While the dismissal of a tenured faculty member is rare, tenured English professor Kay Austen was fired allegedly because she was an advocate for women's rights at the University of Hawaii. According to Austen, her activism put her on a slow-moving and ultimately destructive collision with the university.

The federal district court agreed with Austen's assertions that her department chair—her "implacable enemy," as the judge called him—had rendered her disabled (*Austen v. State of Hawaii*, 759 F. Supp. 612, 618 [D. Haw. 1991]). "I find that Kay Austen has proved by the overwhelming weight of the credible evidence that she was subjected to harassment, retaliation, and discrimination by the University of Hawaii, at first by [her department chair] but thereafter by his superiors who supported him and who participated in the actions," concluded Senior District Judge Samuel P. King (ibid., 622). This ruling came after a decade of litigation that began in 1981. Austen's psychologist testified that when Austen first fell ill in 1981, she was "a woman in great physical pain, psychological pain, and with a badly damaged self esteem. . . . I can say with professional certainty that Kay Austen's experience of [her department chair's] behavior was a direct and major contributing factor to both her state of psychological anguish and to her physical condition. It is unusual for a case to be so clear cut" (ibid., 614).

Austen was hired in 1973 as a 26-year-old promising new hire in the English department and received tenure in 1977. When Austen suffered a back injury in 1981, her department chair doubted and dismissed Austen's medical problems, although several doctors verified the medical nature of her condition. Despite a longstanding policy of granting sick leave and paying faculty full salary for the duration of their illness, the university denied Austen both sick pay and routine sick leave a few months after her disability. Finally in January 1982, she became the first tenured faculty at the university to be terminated. By the time of the court ruling in 1991, Austen had been transformed into a dismissed faculty member and a "permanently and totally disabled" full-time plaintiff (ibid., 613).

Austen construed these life-shattering actions as motivated largely by her ongoing women's rights work within the department. Among other activities, Austen protested the allocation of belittling assignments to women in the department and discrimination against women in hiring and tenure. She organized women in the department into a voting block, held women's meetings, and supported a complaint to federal authorities concerning discrimination against women on campus.

The court reviewed the department chair's behavior toward Austen and Austen's engagement in women's advocacy and concluded, "Discriminatory intent may be inferred from the situation" (ibid., 627). The department chair did not subject male colleagues to the same treatment and, the judge declared, "reasonable women" would construe many of [the department chair's] comments as "typical of males who consider women inferior" (ibid., 628).

The court awarded Austen more than $1.3 million. The university appealed the judgment and lost again in 1992. This victory did not and could not give Austen back what she had lost. Following the litigation, Austen said, "There is no career left here to salvage. There is certainly no sharp young professor called Kay Austen left. There's only the skeleton of the corpse, the facts."

Today Austen lives in Malibu, California, where she writes and counsels plaintiffs facing similar discrimination. She continues to require medical care.

CHAPTER 3

Defenses:
The University's Response

Universities use a variety of strategies to defend themselves in tenure sex discrimination cases. Some institutions delay cases for months or even years, which can exhaust the plaintiff's resources and motivation to pursue the matter. Others file motions for summary judgment, hoping that a judge will throw out the case for insufficient evidence. In other instances, universities reach settlements with plaintiffs to avoid unwanted publicity and legal costs.

Historically, universities have enjoyed special deference from the courts to make employment decisions.

Substantively, universities typically rely on two central arguments: the exceptional nature of the tenure decision and the preservation of academic freedom. Universities contend that the tenure decision is qualitatively different from other employment decisions, and hence they should be permitted exceptional latitude in making such decisions. Because tenure promises extraordinary job security, applying high standards is reasonable, they argue. From the universities' perspective, court oversight of the tenure decision is an infringement on academic freedom. Citing the historic role of universities as guardians of free speech, defending institutions assert that the tenure system should be self regulated and that only academics are qualified to judge each other's fitness for tenure.

Historically, universities have enjoyed special deference from the courts to make employment decisions. Courts have consistently articulated a particular aversion to reviewing tenure decisions, challenging the subjective criteria of tenure, or acting as a "super tenure review committee." See, for example, *Zahorik v. Cornell University*, 729 F.2d 85 (2d Cir. 1984).

Universities have numerous advantages over plaintiffs, including more substantial financial and legal resources, deference from the courts, access to all of the case records, and the ability to redact (edit) the records or withhold them entirely from the plaintiff. Perhaps most importantly, the burden of proof for the university is relatively easy because universities need demonstrate only a legitimate reason for denying tenure. This reason need not be the rationale for the actual decision but simply a plausible reason. Because tenure can be denied for many reasons, constructing a legitimate reason why a candidate *could* be denied tenure is not difficult. In this light, it is not surprising that universities are often able to defend themselves against sex discrimination charges.

Of course many universities defend themselves against sex discrimination charges by adopting fair and consistent employment procedures and sticking to them. Chapter 6 offers recommendations for institutions seeking to prevent sex discrimination in the tenure process.

This chapter describes how university defenses have worked in a variety of circumstances. No attempt is made to evaluate the legitimacy or efficacy of various defense strategies. Rather, the chapter reviews the range of defense strategies with an eye toward implications for the process overall.

Settlements

Many cases are settled rather than won or lost in court. Seven of the 19 LAF plaintiffs described in this report settled their suits (two cases are ongoing). While not commonly thought of as a defense tactic, a settlement defends the university against the costs and unwanted publicity that a lawsuit can bring. The settlement can include a "gag order" prohibiting the plaintiff from discussing specified aspects of the case and further protecting the university. Commenting on Carol Stepien's case (discussed in Chapter 2) against Case Western Reserve University, a department chair described the shared interest among universities to avoid "a messy trial and a media circus, with the kind of national visibility we're not eager to attract" (Mangels 2000, 14).

The director of public relations for the University of Notre Dame described settlement as the first line of defense for the universities:

> **A settlement defends the university against the costs and unwanted publicity that a lawsuit can bring.**

"The first thing we do (in a suit) is determine if we have any liability and if it's a good idea to see if we can reach a settlement" (Heline 1998). If the university concludes that it is not liable for discrimination (and is not, therefore, inclined to settle), it then weighs the cost of going to trial in terms of resources, time, and, presumably, public image. "We are not going to settle just to settle," emphasized the director of public relations (ibid.).

Delays and Technicalities

Delaying tactics are common in tenure lawsuits alleging sex discrimination. Because individual plaintiffs generally have far fewer resources than universities have, delays tend to work in the university's favor. Jacqueline Livingston, a plaintiff in *Zahorik*, wrote vividly about the university's resources. The dean, she recalled, advised Donna Zahorik not to pursue litigation because the university would "destroy her emotionally and financially." He warned her that the university had more time and money than she did and foretold that Cornell would "stall and delay at every possible step and eventually, [Zahorik] would run out of money." According to Livingston, the university "insisted it was prepared to fight to the end, and the cost was immaterial." By 1985 Cornell had spent more than $2.5 million. By comparison, the plaintiffs, whose fundraising tactics included bake sales, raised only $100,000 (Livingston 1985).

The marked disparity between a typical plaintiff's and a university's resources creates a practical incentive for university attorneys to prolong proceedings. Such extra-legal tactics are not confined to universities nor are they illicit—they are part of any lawyer's defense arsenal. Pretrial maneuvers, for example, can take years as defense lawyers delay the production of documents to the extent legal and feasible and extend depositions to create further financial difficulties for plaintiffs and delays in the process.

> *Because individual plaintiffs generally have far fewer resources than universities have, delays tend to work in the university's favor.*

***

Sociology professor Janet Lever's suit against Northwestern University contained a technical issue that needed to be resolved before her substantive charge of sex discrimination could be heard. The technical dispute, raised years after the merits of the case had been developed through discovery, addressed the timeliness of her filing an EEOC complaint. The university argued that the filing period began on May 5, 1980, when the dean notified Lever that she had been denied tenure and offered her a final year of employment. By this standard, Lever's filing of a complaint with the EEOC in June 1981 fell well outside the 300-day statute of limitations.

Lever countered that the dean's May 5 letter did not constitute a decision concerning her tenure denial because in a second letter dated May 14, 1980, the dean, in response to a strongly worded protest from the sociology chair, stated that he would reconsider his recommendation if Lever completed a manuscript by Nov. 1. Lever noted to the provost that Nov. 1 was a few months after the university's six-month deadline to request an appeal by a faculty panel. The provost stated that filing an appeal in May would be inappropriate and Lever could request an appeal after the dean's second decision, should the outcome be negative. Lever submitted the manuscript on time, and it was sent to two reviewers who had not taken part in the first evaluation.

The dean's negative reconsideration decision was communicated to Lever on Jan. 15, 1981. The provost accepted the dean's recommendation and granted an appeals investigation over the dean's objection. Lever thus dated her real tenure denial at Jan. 15, 1981, the date the university's own time clock for appeals began.

The federal district court heard Lever's arguments and ruled against her in 1991. She appealed. The issue on appeal, crucial for all faculty filing discrimination cases, was the timeliness of Lever's filing her charge with the EEOC. To Lever's disappointment, the appeals court affirmed the university's timeline, citing the ruling by the Supreme Court in *Delaware State College v. Ricks*, 449 U.S. 250, 259 (1980), which held that "the limitations periods [sic] commenced to run when the tenure decision was made and [the plaintiff] was notified."

The appeals court stated, "Time starts to run with 'the *discriminatory act*'"—in this case, the denial of tenure—"not the point at which the *consequences* of the act become painful" to the plaintiff (*Lever v. Northwestern University*, 979 F.2d 552, 553 [7th Cir. 1992]), [n.b., emphasis in the original opinion]. By this standard, appeals of the decision or a deferred final date of employment do not postpone the time within which the employee must file a charge. In Lever's case, the court concluded that the dean's original letter "reads more like a decision" and "smacks of finality" (ibid., 554).

This affirmed Northwestern's interpretation that the filing clock commenced when the plaintiff received the letter of rejection from her dean. The Supreme Court denied Lever's appeal in 1993, 13 years after the triggering incident. Lever lost on the technical dispute, and her larger sex discrimination suit was, therefore, never heard.

Lever is now a professor at California State University, Los Angeles.

Motions for Summary Judgment

Filing for the dismissal of a case on summary judgment is another common defense tactic. Either party can initiate a request for summary judgment. In sex discrimination cases involving tenure denial, the defendant—the university—is almost always the party that files the motion.

When a motion for summary judgment is filed, the judge assesses the legal elements of the plaintiff's case and determines whether material (relevant) facts at issue warrant a trial. When judges grant summary judgment for the university, they rule that the plaintiff does not have sufficient material facts to continue the lawsuit. Troublingly for plaintiffs, the number of tenure cases dismissed on summary judgment in recent years has increased.

Indeed, surviving a university's request for summary judgment does not require showing that the plaintiff will win her case, only that she *may* win her case before the judge or jury.

***

Shelley Weinstock taught chemistry at Barnard College from 1985 to 1994 and became eligible for tenure in 1993. Because Barnard is affiliated with Columbia University, the tenure process is particularly complex. Faculty members of the professor's own department must first vote to grant the candidate tenure. If they approve the candidate, the counterpart department at Columbia must then approve her or him. Barnard's president must then vote on tenure and forward the nomination to the provost at Columbia, who convenes a committee to review the candidate. If the provost accepts the committee's positive recommendation, she or he forwards it to the Columbia president and the trustees of both Barnard and Columbia.

Weinstock moved through the first phases of this complex tenure process with relative ease. The chemistry departments of both schools voted for tenure, and Barnard's president moved Weinstock's candidacy forward to Columbia. Things got more complicated when Columbia convened its committee. According to two committee members, the chair uncustomarily contacted them before their meeting and attempted to sow doubts about Weinstock's candidacy. When deliberations began, the dean canvassed members to determine whether the chair's calls had influenced their thinking on Weinstock's candidacy, and the members assured him that the calls had not. After discussions that challenged the quality of Weinstock's research vis-à-vis her counterparts at Columbia, the committee voted 3-2 in favor of tenure—a vote considered "underwhelming [in terms] of support," according to Columbia's president (*Weinstock v. Columbia University*, 224 F.3d 33, 39 [2d Cir. 2000]).

The decision then moved to the provost's desk. He made inquiries to Columbia's chemistry department to clarify the vote, and, as he testified, found that the department thought Weinstein's work "unimaginative" and "had voted to recommend her for tenure as a *courtesy* to their counterpart department at Barnard" (ibid.) [n.b., emphasis in the original opinion]. Thus advised, he testified, he recommended against tenure and did not forward Weinstock's application to the next level of review.

Barnard's dean immediately objected to procedural flaws in the process but to no avail. Weinstock then filed a complaint of sex discrimination in federal district court, and Columbia filed a motion for summary judgment, which was granted. Weinstock appealed the dismissal on summary judgment, and the appellate court reviewed the district court judge's decision *de novo* (as if the evidence and case were being presented for the first time).

Weinstock's case divided the appellate bench. An emphatic majority opinion upheld the district court's granting of summary judgment for Columbia, while Judge Richard J. Cardamone wrote an equally emphatic dissenting opinion. The majority agreed with the lower court that Weinstock would not be able to show that the reasons for denying her tenure were a pretext for discrimination. They rejected Weinstock's assertions that descriptions of her as "nice" and "nurturing" embodied negative gender stereotypes about female scientists (ibid., 53). Weinstock cited procedural irregularities in the tenure process as further evidence of discriminatory intent. While the appellate judges affirmed that such irregularities can raise "a question as to the good faith of the process" (ibid., 45), they found that the phone calls from Columbia's ad hoc committee chair had no impact on the decision making of the committee and that the provost's involvement and inquiries, given the general lack of a clear policy or procedure, did not substantially undermine Columbia's rationale of weak scholarship as a pretext.

As Cardamone summarized in his dissent, "Summary judgment is appropriate only when the [university] has shown that there are no genuine issues of material fact" that should be resolved by a judge or jury. In Cardamone's view, the majority had reviewed matters of fact key to Weinstock's sex discrimination case, resolving ambiguities in favor of Columbia rather than Weinstock (ibid., 56).

Weinstock petitioned the appellate court to review the case en banc. After a two-and-a-half-year delay, the court denied her petition. She then petitioned the Supreme Court. In October 2003 the Supreme Court declined to hear her case, ending her legal battle.

Protection or Withholding of Evidence

Issues of academic freedom have evolved most concretely in cases where universities seek to protect or withhold evidence from confidential tenure review processes. If they have trouble obtaining tenure review materials, plaintiffs cannot easily determine whether they have been treated fairly. Universities argue that disclosing these materials would inhibit the honest evaluation of candidates because reviewers will write candidly about tenure candidates only under conditions of anonymity. Lack of confidentiality, they argue, would unduly compromise the tenure process and, therefore, the free exchange and development of ideas.

> *If they have trouble obtaining tenure review materials, plaintiffs cannot easily determine whether they have been treated fairly.*

The U.S. Supreme Court opinion *University of Pennsylvania v. EEOC*, 493 U.S. 182 (1990), challenged the university's privilege to maintain confidentiality and resolved some of the ambiguity evident in federal circuit court rulings. The Court clarified that a university is not exempt from the Title VII requirement of disclosure of relevant materials to the EEOC, asserting that a "university does not enjoy a special privilege" to withhold peer review materials once their "mere relevance" has been established by the requesting party (*University of Pennsylvania*, 182). The Court held that the EEOC could subpoena employers (universities) who refused to provide the material voluntarily. Despite this important ruling, universities continue to assert the confidentiality of tenure files in discrimination lawsuits. Below are two examples of how courts have addressed this thorny issue.

***

Religious studies professor Diana Paul, whose case is also described in Chapter 2, characterized her sex and race discrimination case against Stanford University as a dispute within a dispute. Her primary dispute regarding denial of tenure and promotion embedded a second dispute: denial of access to information in her personnel file. Paul argued that she could develop her primary suit only through access to these records. She opined that by invoking the veil of secrecy around the peer review process, universities have been able to effectively limit the promotion of women.

Access to peer review letters in her file was critical to Paul's case, so she filed a motion to compel discovery. Stanford argued in its defense that academic freedom and privileges protected them from having to disclose confidential letters. The judge reviewed case law on disclosure of confidential materials and voiced skepticism toward Stanford's—and other universities'—longstanding defense that reviewers will write candidly only under conditions of anonymity:

> It can be non-laughably argued that reviewers who know that their identity might be disclosed will neither refuse to comment nor retreat into useless abstractions or disingenuous flattery, but, instead, will articulate their opinions, and describe the bases for them, with greater precision and better developed logic. Judges, like professors making tenure decisions, regularly are called upon to make difficult decisions. The legal system has accepted the notion that the quality of those difficult decisions will be better if judges are compelled to disclose the bases on which they rule. Judges' decisions virtually always disappoint

someone. . . . These considerations lead this court to
ascribe somewhat less weight than it otherwise might to
the interest the University says would be damaged if plaintiff had access to the substance of the evaluations in her
tenure review file. (*Paul v. Stanford University*, 1986 WL 614,
2 [N.D. Cal. 1986])

The judge acknowledged that the rejected candidate must make
some showing of justification before receiving access to her files. In
other words, the judge needed to consider the viability of Paul's
charges as well as the importance of the peer reviews to her case.
Finding good evidence of a prima facie case, the judge crafted a compromise solution and appointed a special master, "someone acceptable
to both parties, with substantial experience in related academic matters, to prepare *full* summaries of the material in plaintiff's tenure file,"
at Stanford's expense (ibid., 8) [n.b., emphasis in the original opinion].
Paul settled in 1986 and received $54,000.

***

The need for an outsider's perspective can also be seen in Anne
Margolis's case against Williams College. In the school's internal
appeals process, Margolis was first required to appeal the tenure-
denial decision to the committee on promotions and reappointment
and the dean of faculty, who had participated in the initial decision,
and who, as might be expected, denied Margolis's appeal. She then
petitioned the faculty steering committee for reconsideration, but its
chair, according to Margolis, made it clear that the appeal was strictly
procedural and would not address substantive issues. At no point in
the appeals process was she given access to her personnel or tenure
files nor was she allowed legal representation.

Margolis then filed a complaint with the Massachusetts
Commission Against Discrimination. MCAD found probable cause
to hear the case and ordered the college to turn over roughly 100 faculty tenure files saying, "The heart of proving this case of discrimination is comparative evidence" (*Margolis v. Williams College*,
Petitioner's memorandum, 3). Williams denied the charges and

refused to turn over the files, claiming academic freedom considerations. The college appealed to a single justice of the Massachusetts Supreme Judicial Court and lost. Williams was in the process of filing a second appeal to the full court when the U.S. Supreme Court issued its unanimous decision in *University of Pennsylvania v. EEOC*, 493 U.S. 182 (1990), holding that the First Amendment does not shield academic employers from having to turn over tenure files.

The college's substantive defense was that Margolis did not meet the institution's exacting standards for tenure. According to Margolis, the acting chair told her that her prize-winning dissertation was so "shockingly bad" that it would never be published (n.b., it was selected for publication just weeks after Margolis was denied tenure). The college distinguished between competency to teach or conduct research and truly outstanding achievement worthy of tenure. The faculty handbook specified strict standards for tenure, including "exceptional strength" in teaching and scholarship and "significant contributions" to the college community. "Promotion to tenure is by no means automatic," the college's attorneys wrote, "and only a minority of assistant professors achieve it" (*Margolis v. Williams College*, Answer, February 10, 1987, 1).

Williams College attempted to explain the contradiction between earlier, positive appraisals of Margolis's scholarship and the ultimately negative tenure decision by asserting that criteria are far more demanding for "final tenure decisions" than for reappointment or promotion at a lower level (ibid., 2). In essence, the college insisted that Margolis's scholarship and teaching simply failed to meet the exceptional strength standard.

Margolis claimed that because of her pregnancy, which had caused her to shift to part-time tenure track, and her women's studies scholarship, the college had held her to a higher standard than it held similarly situated males. She also maintained that her case hinged on inaccurate assessments of her scholarly promise, especially since a senior faculty member in her department refused to review the revised version of her dissertation prior to her tenure review.

By the time her case settled in 1991, Margolis had completed law school. She now practices family law, specializing in representing victims of domestic violence.

Claiming Academic Freedom

If the university opts to forego or forestall settlement negotiations with the plaintiff or if she does not want to settle, the university's attorneys must prepare a trial defense. This defense often draws formally and informally on the principle of academic freedom and the special status of the university in U.S. culture. Using the defense of academic freedom, universities assert a right to fire and hire without oversight from the courts.

> *Using the defense of academic freedom, universities assert a right to fire and hire without oversight from the courts.*

The courts have long recognized individual and institutional academic freedom. In *Sweezy v. State of New Hampshire by Wyman*, 354 U.S. 234, 263 (1957), Justice Felix Frankfurter, concurring with the majority, quoted four essential freedoms of a university: "to determine for itself on academic grounds who may teach, what may be taught, how it shall be taught, and who may be admitted to study." Frankfurter's articulation of academic freedom for universities was embraced in several rulings, but the scope and extent of academic freedom in tenure decisions has not yet been clearly delineated.

In tenure cases, the special deference that universities enjoy as guardians of academic freedom can make courts reticent to intervene in academic employment decisions. *Faro v. New York University*, 502 F.2d 1229 (2d Cir. 1974), illustrates the special deference paid to universities in early sex discrimination suits. After ridiculing the plaintiff for "envision[ing] herself as a modern Jeanne d'Arc fighting for the rights of embattled womanhood on an academic battlefield, facing a solid phalanx of men and male faculty prejudice," the judge opined, "Of all fields which the federal courts should hesitate to invade and take over, education and faculty appointments at a University level are probably the least suited for federal court supervision" (*Faro v. NYU*, 1231).

By the 1980s, some circuit courts began to challenge the notion that universities should receive special protection in hiring decisions. In *Brown v. Trustees of Boston University*, 891 F.2d 337, 360 (1st Cir. 1989), the appeals court concluded, "Academic freedom does not include the freedom to discriminate against tenure candidates on the basis of sex or other impermissible grounds."

Today, courts are less likely to defer to universities solely on the basis of academic freedom. Yet hesitancy to thrash around in the "sacred groves of academe . . . looking for possible . . . gender bias" persists (*Bickerstaff v. Vassar College*, 992 F. Supp. 372, 377 [S.D.N.Y. 1998]).

***

Zahorik v. Cornell University, 729 F.2d 85 (2d Cir. 1984) tackled important philosophical issues in academic sex discrimination cases, including the interplay of academic freedom and a plaintiff's rights as an employee. In this case, a group of female faculty and coaches brought a class action lawsuit against Cornell University in 1981 alleging sex discrimination in promotion and pay. Of the original "Cornell Eleven," five pursued the lawsuit alleging that they had been discriminated against in tenure evaluations.

The court of appeals detailed how tenure decisions and the academic context differ from other professional settings: "Tenure decisions in an academic setting involve a combination of factors which tend to set them apart from employment decisions generally." First, the court noted, it entails a lifelong commitment, and thus employers should be given great latitude in their deliberations. Second, tenure decisions "are often non-competitive" such that comparisons among candidates are difficult to make, and third, the process is "usually highly decentralized" (*Zahorik v. Cornell University*, 92).

Cornell proved tenacious, claiming that a speedy settlement would create a precedent that could adversely affect the university's reputation. After 230 people, including many Cornell faculty members, signed a petition supporting the plaintiffs, the Cornell president wrote a response stressing the importance of tenure for academic freedom and excellence: "Tenure review . . . is fundamental to the character of the university. The distinction that Cornell has achieved in the academic world is due largely to the quality and integrity of the faculty" (Rhodes responds, 1981).

The university's early legal victories drew heavily on the academic freedom defense. In the first legal round, Cornell filed a motion for dismissal on summary judgment and won. The plaintiffs appealed the ruling, but an appellate court upheld it in a decision that outlined judicial concerns about academic freedom and interference with the peculiar rituals of tenure.

Cornell eventually agreed to pay a $250,000 settlement in 1984.

CHAPTER 4

Burdens: Proving Lies and Discrimination

The plaintiff bears the ultimate burden of proving her case of sex discrimination throughout the course of the litigation. Under the *McDonnell Douglas* paradigm (see Chapter 1), the plaintiff must show that the university's rationale is, in fact, a lie or pretext to cover discriminatory intent and motive. Alternatively, under the *Price Waterhouse* standard (see Chapter 1), the plaintiff can present a mixed-motive case, using direct evidence that gender was a motivating factor in the university's decision. In a mixed-motive case, sex discrimination does not necessarily have to be the only factor in the university's decision, but it must be an important factor. As a practical matter, plaintiffs often allege both pretext and mixed motives at the outset of the case.

> *The burden of proof for plaintiffs is onerous.*

As the two cases below illustrate, the burden of proof for plaintiffs is onerous. Neither proving that the university lied about its stated reason for rejecting the tenure candidate nor demonstrating that the tenure denial was unfair is sufficient. The highly subjective criteria for tenure make it relatively easy for universities to point to unseemly but not illegal reasons for their actions. Faculty on a tenure committee can assert that the candidate was not collegial, which can be permissible grounds for tenure denial, or they can marshal evidence of other issues not rooted in sex to deflect the core charge of sex discrimination.

***

In a closely watched and influential case dealing with the issue of pretext, Cynthia Fisher eventually lost her lawsuit against Vassar College. Alleging that Vassar had discriminated against her based on her sex, marital status, and age, Fisher prevailed in her first trial, proving to Federal District Court Judge Constance Baker Motley that Fisher was equally or more qualified for tenure than comparable scholars and using statistics to show that Vassar had a history of not granting tenure to married women.

Vassar countered that Fisher's scholarship did not meet the standards for tenure and tried, unsuccessfully, to introduce its own statistics concerning married women and tenure. Motley agreed that Vassar's reasons for denying Fisher tenure were pretextual: "The termination of plaintiff's employment resulted not from any inadequacy of her performance or qualifications or service, but from the pretextual and bad faith evaluation by Vassar of her qualifications" (*Fisher v. Vassar College*, 852 F. Supp. 1193, 1218 [S.D.N.Y. 1994]). The court ordered Vassar to reinstate Fisher and to pay $626,000 in damages.

Vassar appealed the federal district court's ruling, arguing that Fisher had failed to undermine as pretextual Vassar's legitimate reasons for denying her tenure, including negative departmental reports on her originality, scholarship, service, and unique contributions to the biology curriculum. Vassar argued its first appeal before three judges who wrestled with the question of pretext in their ruling, reversing in part and vacating Fisher's district court victory. Citing the Supreme Court's decision in *St. Mary's Honor Center v. Hicks*, 509 U.S. 502 (1993), the court underscored that Fisher had to prove by a "preponderance of evidence" not only that Vassar had dissembled in its rationale for denying her tenure but also that it was trying specifically to disguise sex discrimination (*Fisher v. Vassar College*, 70 F.3d 1420, 1433 [2d Cir. 1995]). The court wrote that it is "the plaintiff's burden to demonstrate (a) that the College's explanation for denial of tenure was false and pretextual and (b) that the real reason for denial was discrimination based on either sex or sex plus marriage" (ibid., 1434).

The district court had concluded that the biology department's tenure report on Fisher was pretextual and "made in bad faith . . . and represented the application of patently discriminatory standards" (*Fisher v. Vassar College*, 852 F. Supp. 1193, 1209 [S.D.N.Y. 1994]). Among other examples, Motley pointed to distortions of Fisher's record in the tenure report to support the conclusion that Vassar had generated a pretext for denying Fisher tenure. These included a charge that Fisher had not used her sabbatical year wisely for research when in fact Fisher had spent nine months out of that year in a laboratory; collaborated with several different groups of scientists; submitted eight grant proposals, six of which were funded; published one manuscript and written another; and presented papers at national and international meetings. Motley also found that the biology department had distorted Fisher's teaching recommendations by "selectively exclud[ing] favorable ratings and focus[ing] on the two courses in which Dr. Fisher had difficulties" (ibid.).

The appellate judges agreed that Fisher had demonstrated a prima facie case of discrimination and that the lower court had reasonably and without clear error interpreted the tenure material as pretextual. The appellate court emphasized, however, that a prima facie case and the establishment of pretext does not amount to a finding of liability for discrimination and thus disagreed with the district court's interpretation of the weight assigned to pretext, saying, "The finding of pretext here did not alone justify a finding of discrimination" (*Fisher v. Vassar College*, 70 F.3d 1420, 1437 [2d Cir. 1995]). Quoting *Hicks*, the appellate court reminded the district court, "That the employer's proffered reason is unpersuasive, or even obviously contrived, does not necessarily establish that the plaintiff's proffered reason of race [or sex, in this case] is correct" (ibid., 1438).

The appellate judges conceded that although "there are cases in which discriminatory intent is the only probable reason for the employer's proffer of a pretextual reason to the court," that was not the situation in this case (ibid., 1437). The court reviewed the evidence relied upon by the district court as well as other evidence offered by Fisher at trial and determined that it did not support a finding that Vassar had a policy of discriminating against married women or that Vassar discriminated against Fisher based on her sex. The court also found error in the district court's reliance on the statistics presented by the plaintiff to support a finding of discrimination. Fisher had pointed out that no married woman had ever been tenured in the hard sciences in the college's 130-year history.

Fisher's attorney requested an en banc hearing (a hearing before the full appellate court). The court upheld the earlier appellate ruling and revisited the question of pretext. Defining pretext as "a proffered reason that is not credited by the finder of fact (i.e, the judge)," the en banc opinion clarified that the establishment of pretext, as in the Fisher case, "does not answer the question: pretext for what?" The court noted that decision makers may dissemble for "small-minded" but nondiscriminatory reasons such as "back-scratching, … institutional politics, envy, nepotism, spite, or personal hostility." While unattractive, these reasons are not discriminatory per se. "In short, the fact that the proffered reason was false does not necessarily mean that the true motive was the illegal one argued by the plaintiff" (*Fisher v. Vassar College*, 114 F.3d 1332, 1337 [2d Cir. 1997]).

The en banc ruling summarized that pretext alone cannot establish the plaintiff's discrimination case. A finding of pretext may "advance" the plaintiff's case if other evidence also suggests discrimination, but it cannot carry the day for the plaintiff unless she shows by a "preponderance of evidence" that the pretext hid discrimination (ibid., 1333). This judicial interpretation made it more difficult for future plaintiffs to win sex discrimination cases without a "smoking gun." As Fisher pointed out, most academics are too smart to make statements such as "married women should stay home and take care of their families."

Fisher appealed to the U.S. Supreme Court, which refused to hear her case. Today Fisher is on the faculty at the University of Illinois at Urbana/Champaign.

The battle between sociology professor Rona Fields and Clark University revolved around the question of pretext as well as direct evidence. Fields first filed a complaint against the university with the Massachusetts Commission Against Discrimination and the EEOC in 1975. During the next 15 years, her case was interpreted and reinterpreted several times in the federal courts.

Fields joined the staff of Clark University in 1972 after receiving several job offers in the flush of enthusiasm for the new field of women's studies. According to Fields, the university offered her the tantalizing opportunity to begin programs in women's and Irish studies at the university, so she opted to move across the country.

Fields's career took off during her early years at the university. An expert on intergenerational and intercommunal violence, she traveled to Ireland and stayed during the violent and politically tumultuous summer of 1972 to gather data for a book. When she returned, the media sought her for interviews on the Irish conflict, and her profile as a scholar and speaker began to grow.

Fields found her colleagues at Clark surprisingly indifferent, if not hostile, to her accomplishments. In her lawsuit, she charged that the chair of her department competed with her. Fields contended that the university forced her to resign from two American Psychological Association bodies she had helped establish concerning women and social and ethical responsibility. She alleged that she was assigned heavier teaching loads involving more preparation time than were her male colleagues and that she was sexually harassed by a senior faculty member who eventually cast a vote against her tenure. Ironically, Fields's prestige and reputation outside the university grew as her status at the university diminished and became more precarious.

Meanwhile, many of the university's initial promises to Fields—which Clark denied making—evaporated. When she did not receive funding to begin programs in either women's studies or Irish studies, the university pleaded budget restrictions. Fields believed that the university had promised her tenure upon the publication of her first book and was disappointed when her bid for tenure in 1974 was denied. After unsuccessful university appeals, Fields filed an EEOC complaint and left Clark in 1976. Fields filed her first Title VII lawsuit against the university in 1980 after the EEOC issued a finding of probable cause on her sex discrimination charges.

This began a legal odyssey that would continue into the 1990s. Fields scored a victory at the federal district court level in 1986 when the judge concluded that the department of sociology "was generally permeated with sexual discrimination of which the plaintiff was in fact a victim" (*Fields v. Clark University*, 1986 WL 5350, 6 [D. Mass. 1986]). The judge ordered Fields reinstated for a two-year probationary period and the payment of back salary, yet the university resisted reinstatement until ordered to do so. Fields, predictably, found herself shunned by the department upon her return. She alleged that her colleagues blackballed her, making it difficult for her to find another academic appointment.

Clark appealed, and in 1987 the federal appeals court vacated the lower court's ruling and remanded the case for a new trial before a new judge. The appellate ruling was significant because it foreshadowed the alternate Title VII process established by the Supreme Court in *Price Waterhouse v. Hopkins*, 490 U.S. 228 (1989). The *Fields* appellate ruling and *Price Waterhouse* both re-examined the burden of proof for defendants when the plaintiff produces direct evidence of discrimination.

In *Fields v. Clark University*, 817 F.2d 931, 935 (1st Cir. 1987), the appellate court agreed with the district court's conclusion that "strong evidence of a pervasively sexist attitude on the part of the male members of the sociology department" amounted to "direct evidence" of sex discrimination. The court found that in cases where direct evidence of discrimination exists, the courts should not "slavishly follow" (ibid., 936) the *McDonnell Douglas* framework. With direct evidence of discrimination, the appellate court determined, the burden is on the employer to prove by a preponderance of the evidence that "the same decision would have been made absent the discrimination" (ibid.). According to the appellate court, "The district court's finding that sexual discrimination 'impermissibly infected' the decision not to grant Fields tenure appears to us to be the equivalent of a finding that she proved by direct evidence that discrimination was a motivating factor in the decision" (ibid., 937). The appellate court also found, however, that the district court erred by reinstating Fields for two years and awarding back pay without a finding that the university failed to carry its burden to prove that Fields would not have been granted tenure absent discrimination.

In the early phases of the new trial in federal district court, the question of pretext resurfaced. In his opening statement, Fields's lawyer described several members of the sociology department as "obviously interested, not impartial reviewers . . . but actually people who stand to gain and benefit themselves by recommending against . . . tenure." The judge interrupted and cautioned, "Now that's not the basis for any claim under Title VII, is it? That is, it won't do you any good to prove that their votes were self-serving and various such things. You've got to prove sex discrimination." Fields's lawyer responded, "I understand that, but I'm trying to explain the mechanism," to which the judge cautioned, "Well, I'm just wondering if you're not weakening your claim by telling me there are a lot of other reasons" why Fields's colleagues would view her unfavorably (*Fields v. Clark University*, Transcript, Day 3, III-41 [December 21, 1990]).

Clark seized on the question of pretext and argued that Fields had not debunked the university's rationale for denying her tenure—bad teaching—as pretextual. After Fields testified and rested her case, the university's attorneys filed a motion to dismiss Fields's complaint. They argued that Fields's allegations did not amount to a prima facie case that would, in turn, compel Clark to present a defense. Furthermore, they argued, she failed to demonstrate that the university's reason for her tenure denial was a pretext for discrimination.

In particular, Clark's attorneys noted that Fields had discerned a variety of motives for her tenure denial, a number of which were "wholly *unrelated* to the plaintiff's gender" (*Fields v. Clark University*, Memorandum of defendant, 7 [December 27, 1990]) [n.b., emphasis in the original opinion]. For example, Fields argued that three members of the department may have denied her tenure because they felt that a favorable decision for her would decrease their own prospects for obtaining tenure. "While plaintiff's contention may lead to the inference that these three professors had a theoretical conflict of interest," Clark argued, "her allegations negate any basis for finding that . . . [they] were motivated to deny plaintiff tenure because of her sex" (ibid.). In her testimony, Fields also introduced the possibility that another faculty member opposed her because of her political ideology, but Clark's attorneys were quick to point out, "This alleged ideological motivation . . . does not violate Title VII" (ibid., 8). Other faculty objected to Fields's focus on Ireland, she testified, but this did not link the tenure denial to gender bias.

The university suggested that insofar as pretext existed in its tenure review, it hid unseemly motives unrelated to gender:

> There may well be personal animus between the plaintiff and [the department chair], but there is no evidence of gender bias. He hired her, after all, knowing she was a woman and, on her testimony, in part because of it. . . . He may have come to dislike her. She said it was because their political views were incompatible, but that has nothing to do with gender bias. (*Fields v. Clark University*, Transcript, Day 3, III-9 [December 21, 1990])

Yet Fields did have the unrebutted incident of what her lawyers characterized as quid pro quo sexual harassment: a senior professor's comment that Fields's refusal of his sexual advances was "no way to get tenure." In their opposition to Clark's motion to dismiss, Fields's attorneys emphasized this incident as a compelling piece of the puzzle. Clark dealt with the evidence of harassment by arguing that the incident was "greatly embellished" and perhaps a "recent contrivance," but in any case they put his vote aside because the vote did not matter in the final tenure decision (ibid.).

After Fields's testimony and Clark's motion for dismissal, the judge had to determine whether Fields had, indeed, presented direct evidence of sex discrimination. If she convinced the judge that she had done so, the burden would shift to Clark to show that even if it had not discriminated, it would have made the same decision. Ultimately the judge was not convinced that Fields had direct evidence of discrimination, yet neither did he grant Clark's motion to dismiss the case because Fields would not be able to establish a prima facie case or undo Clark's decision as pretextual. The judge confessed confusion regarding the *Price Waterhouse* decision and the 1st Circuit ruling about what constitutes direct evidence. Although he felt that the motion to dismiss had validity, he did not think it "wise . . . to send the case back to the Court of Appeals with a risk for the parties and the court system of a third round of this already ancient case" (*Fields v. Clark University*, Transcript, Day 4, IV-2 [January 25, 1991]). By the time of this decision, 15 years had elapsed since Fields filed her first EEOC complaint.

The judge proceeded with the trial, which Fields lost. The 1991 decision, coming in the post–*Price Waterhouse* era, reiterated that mixed-motive cases are different from pretext cases. The court found, however, that Fields had not satisfied her burden to demonstrate a prima facie case of sex discrimination under either the *Price Waterhouse* or *McDonnell Douglas* analyses. Fields appealed the second trial verdict on several grounds, but the appellate court upheld the district court's ruling.

Attorneys for Fields then filed an appeal with the U.S. Supreme Court. One of the more significant issues entailed the interpretation of direct evidence under *Price Waterhouse*. Fields's attorneys hoped that the Supreme Court would use their case to hone the concept of direct evidence and provide much-needed guidance to the lower federal courts grappling with discrimination in employment. The Supreme Court did not hear Fields's case, and her decades-long tenure battle with Clark University ended in 1993.

Despite continued recognition as an important scholar in her field, Fields has not obtained an academic appointment since her position at Clark University ended.

CHAPTER 5

Aftermath: The Costs and Rewards of Litigation

The odds in sex discrimination cases do not favor plaintiffs. In most sex discrimination cases that reach trial, universities win. Many cases do not reach trial because they are dropped or resolved during the litigation process. Of the 19 AAUW Legal Advocacy Fund–supported cases described in this report, eight (42 percent) plaintiffs lost, seven (37 percent) settled, two (11 percent) won, and two cases are ongoing.

This chapter examines the outcomes of these cases from a legal, financial, and emotional point of view. Highlighting the voices of LAF-supported plaintiffs, the chapter illustrates the profound impact of litigation on plaintiffs' personal and professional lives. The process of suing a university for sex discrimination can exact a heavy toll on plaintiffs and their families. But, as so many of the LAF-supported plaintiffs found, the process does have intangible rewards that come from doing what one believes is right. And while the legal process can be financially and emotionally draining, it can also empower plaintiffs. Regardless of the outcome, many plaintiffs found that fighting the good fight was worthwhile in and of itself—for themselves and for other women.

> *Regardless of the outcome, many plaintiffs found that fighting the good fight was worthwhile in and of itself—for themselves and for other women.*

Legal Outcomes

Many LAF plaintiffs settled their cases out of court. Most settlement agreements include confidentiality clauses that prohibit the plaintiff from discussing the specific terms of the settlement or, in some cases, the details of her suit. In the limited number of LAF-supported cases in which attorneys and plaintiffs could disclose specific information about the settlement terms, some plaintiffs received sizeable financial settlements that included compensation for emotional distress and injury as well as front and back pay and reinstatement or tenure. Religious studies professor Diana Paul (see Chapters 2 and 3) was awarded more than $50,000 in her settlement against Stanford University, and Margaretta Lovell (see Chapter 2) received tenure at the University of California, Berkeley as a result of her suit.

Many plaintiffs see their settlements as victories. Although the financial terms were confidential, Anne Margolis (see Chapter 3) reported that she was satisfied with her settlement against Williams College and described the money as "substantial." She had some ambivalence about missing her day in court but settled in part because of her "family's desire for closure, especially given the many delays in reaching trial and the prospect of lengthy appeals by the college should we have prevailed." Margolis and her lawyer welcomed the settlement with Williams as a "vindication of [her] reasons for filing suit," particularly since this agreement did not bar Margolis from discussing aspects of her case other than the actual monetary settlement.

> *Many plaintiffs see their settlements as victories.*

On the other hand, some plaintiffs feel that a settlement is a defeat. Jacqueline Livingston, one of the plaintiffs in *Zahorik v. Cornell University* viewed settlement with the university as the end of a dream. "I had dreamed of justice, social reform and professional equity for women," she wrote. "Instead, I felt I was simply being 'paid off' [with the equivalent of one year's salary], and nothing would be remedied." The lengthy process left Livingston feeling "violated, battered and maligned" (Livingston 1985, 5).

The potential costs and rewards of trials differ from those of settlement, for both universities and plaintiffs. The Civil Rights Act of 1991 gives plaintiffs litigating under Title VII the right to demand a jury trial. Some lawyers argue that plaintiffs fare better in a jury trial, and the advantages of a jury trial may have grown with the conservative judicial appointments of the 1980s, early 1990s, and today. "Historically, juries have been . . . more sympathetic to employee claims than judges [have]," wrote lawyer Martha West (1994, 123). Regardless of the outcome, a trial can generate negative publicity that may roil faculty, alumni, donors, national organizations, and other constituents.

For many plaintiffs, going to trial presents the best opportunity to publicly disclose their experiences with discrimination, even if they are not victorious. When the University of Kentucky offered biology professor Ricky Hirschhorn (see Chapter 2) a pretrial monetary settlement, she opted for a jury trial so that she could publicly discuss the university's treatment of her and have her day in court. In the end, the jury ruled against Hirschhorn, who lost a subsequent appeal as well. Having one's day in court may be appealing from a psychological standpoint, but a trial is always risky.

Financial Costs

Lawsuits can be time-consuming and expensive, and tenure cases are no exception. Litigation expenses, the most quantifiable and literal cost to the plaintiff, are daunting, especially for untenured academicians who do not enjoy substantial salaries vis-à-vis their peers in business, law, medicine, or other professions. Plaintiffs whose lawyers bill hourly are shocked at how quickly basic research, correspondence, and filing fees can deplete their savings and financial resources. The least costly lawsuit was estimated at $20,000 for a case that settled out of court. Other cases, including Beth Kern's against the University of Notre Dame (see Chapter 2), tallied more than $170,000. Most plaintiffs reported legal expenses between

Litigation is not for the poor.

$50,000 and $100,000. "Litigation is not for the poor," concluded a plaintiff who found the financial obligations to be "the most daunting. I didn't file suit to make money. . . . To call it frightening is a great understatement. The financial risks are nightmarish."

Plaintiffs fund their lawsuits through a variety of means. Financial support from the Legal Advocacy Fund usually covers only a small percentage of legal expenses. Some plaintiffs receive financial help from supporters at their university, community organizations, local businesswomen, or others sympathetic to their cause. For most plaintiffs the bulk of the money comes from their own and their families' personal reserves and savings. Kern covered her legal costs of $170,000 through "self funding [during] a booming stock market." Another plaintiff took out a second mortgage, used savings, and sold family heirlooms on consignment.

"Be prepared to place yourself at substantial financial risk," Kern cautions prospective plaintiffs. For most plaintiffs this financial risk invariably affects their entire families and may cause guilt or tension in relationships. One plaintiff found "putting the welfare and security of my family in jeopardy" the most difficult aspect of her case. Since many of her assets were held jointly with her husband, she could find no way to be solely responsible for the debts incurred during her suit. The financial risks of litigation created anxiety, guilt, and "periodic bouts of fear" throughout the family.

One plaintiff contrasted her hard-won resources "that my husband and I have struggled to save over the years" with those of the university and the state behind it. Janet Lever (see Chapter 3) concluded that the deep pockets of a university make it a formidable opponent. Financially, litigation against a university typically pits David against Goliath. While plaintiffs become increasingly distraught, according to one plaintiff, "as the financial burden [gets] higher and higher . . . knowing that I was risking our life's savings," the university can afford to "run up the costs."

A plaintiff's financial distress may encourage her to settle or drop the case entirely. Universities, in contrast, have legal departments versed in university policy and relevant employment law, the financial wherewithal to supplement that counsel with outside support as necessary, and, in many cases, a well-heeled alumni base that might donate to the university's defense. Universities in state systems have the additional legal resources of the state, and all universities with stature in their communities are likely to enjoy informal connections and networks with legislators, legal professionals, and the business community.

The Personal and Professional Price Tag

As high as the financial burden can be for plaintiffs in a sex discrimination case, other costs reach far beyond a plaintiff's wallet. Former plaintiff Catherine Clinger (see Chapter 2) described the emotional toil, warning those considering litigation to expect "to be as depressed as you've ever been in your life, to realize that you see things that are really obvious and it will take a long time to convince someone else. . . . And you should go in knowing that there is a huge possibility that you will get nothing but grief out of this." Others described what it is like to be a plaintiff in the academic context as "nightmarish," "a journey to hell and back," and "traumatic." One simply commented, "It has made me sad."

Rejected tenure applicants have a long way to fall. They move from seeing themselves as competent professionals on the cusp of tenure and lifelong employment to hearing that they are unworthy of tenure and slated for dismissal from the university, usually within one year of the decision. Losing a job can be devastating for anyone, but it is particularly difficult for highly specialized professionals. A professor in medieval literature, for example, would be hard-pressed to find employment in her field outside academia.

Rejected tenure applicants have a long way to fall.

Finding a position at another university can be difficult. News of a tenure denial spreads rapidly in the insular worlds of academic disciplines. Some schools may hesitate to hire someone rejected for tenure by another school—even by a highly ranked university.

In today's crowded academic job market, rejected tenure candidates face an uphill battle.

Once a lawsuit is filed, many plaintiffs are labeled "troublemakers" by their small academic community. This label further exacerbates the search for a new academic appointment. Professors inhabit a small pond in their discipline and even a smaller pond in their sub-specialty and area of expertise. In some areas only a handful of professors work on themes of particular interest to the plaintiff. Plaintiffs who pursue other academic jobs may find themselves stymied by negative formal or informal references from the university they sued and their former colleagues.

Janet Lever, who lost her case in a statute of limitations battle, found that being labeled a troublemaker was the most difficult aspect of being a litigant: "It makes getting other academic appointments more difficult. Because it's understood that deans won't trust you, faculty search committees don't waste scarce resources recruiting you." Another plaintiff agreed: "The troublemaker label is difficult to deal with. It taints all levels of your professional life at the university, communities, grant proposals, support for projects," and so on. When one's fate rests so squarely in the hands of a few individuals, opting for legal action against one of the big players is essentially opting out of the profession.

In the tightly knit academic community, reverberations of a lawsuit can be painful on a personal as well as a professional level. Many professors derive a sense of identity from their work, and many have long-standing friendships from graduate school, conferences, and professional associations. Once a lawsuit is filed, some plaintiffs find themselves pariahs to colleagues with whom, just a few weeks earlier, they had enjoyed amiable professional relationships. For some plaintiffs, the devastation of professional ties and collegiality is one of the most surprising and heartbreaking aspects of their litigation. One plaintiff stated, "There are people who will not talk to me . . . people who are afraid to talk to me (they've told me so) . . . some clearly find it uncomfortable to be seen talking to me." She noted, as did other plaintiffs, "Friends *outside* the university provide the most support." Diana Paul said, "Of course, no one in the department would talk to me" after she sued, and Catherine Clinger found that "many people [I] once had a comfortable acquaintance with no longer contact me." She was most surprised by the extent to which administrators "neglect the greater good in order to protect [their] own . . . self-interests."

For some plaintiffs, the devastation of professional ties and collegiality is one of the most surprising and heartbreaking aspects of their litigation.

Plaintiffs expressed particular dismay that women colleagues, both tenured and untenured, were not more supportive. Among the greatest disappointments of litigation, according to one plaintiff, was "how some people—including women—will walk away from you." Janet Lever bemoaned "lack of support from women who also blame the victim more than they see sexism in the system," and another plaintiff found that some colleagues, "including many women, avoided or even seemed to shun me." Diana Paul agreed that the greatest surprise of litigation was discovering "who had the courage to step forward to tell the facts and who had no sense of responsibility or interest [in being] a witness."

Once litigation is under way, the university's defense invariably will include documentation of the plaintiff's shortcomings in scholarship, teaching, or service or negative assessments from her colleagues or external reviewers. The university produces these items to show legitimate, nondiscriminatory reasons for its decision and tries to show the candidate's scholarship and personality in the least favorable light. Of course, a lawsuit is an adversarial action, and institutions can be expected to put their best foot forward by highlighting the plaintiff's weaknesses. Still, hearing her alleged shortcomings is a notably unpleasant experience for the plaintiff.

As described in Chapter 4, Vassar College's protracted defense against Cynthia Fisher's discrimination allegations hinged on the core argument that her colleagues simply did not like her and did not want to develop a lifelong professional relationship with her. Other plaintiffs read reviews that contained stinging criticisms of their scholarly work. For plaintiffs enmeshed in depositions or a trial, the experience can become a Kafkaesque ordeal of listening to unflattering critiques of their personalities and professional abilities stated for the public record and then elaborated and dissected by legal adversaries. One plaintiff described the process as humiliating.

Lawsuits can affect all aspects of a plaintiff's life, in part simply because they are time-consuming. Plaintiffs who involve themselves in the preparation of their cases and who work closely with lawyers stand a greater chance of success, but this entails taking on a second, ad hoc profession as a litigant, with all of the conflicts and time commitments that suggests. Catherine Clinger wished in retrospect that she had been a "lazier plaintiff," because she involved herself deeply in time-consuming legal preparation through the entire process at the expense of other interests. Diana Paul found balancing time spent in litigation with the demands of parenting and working to be the most difficult aspect of her case. Litigation left her feeling distracted and more "self-absorbed because the litigation required so much of my time and emotional energy." Another plaintiff most regretted the lost years with her husband. Her case, which eventually settled, lasted seven years. "My life and my husband's life were consumed by the litigation. Those years—and what we might have done together—are gone forever," she said.

Emotionally, many plaintiffs discussed in this report experienced a roller coaster of conflicting and strong reactions to the litigation process, beginning with shock and bewilderment, moving to bitterness and anger, and ending with a resolute commitment to tell their story or act. "Find ways to deal with anger, resentment, and bitterness, because all of those ugly emotions will rear their heads," one plaintiff advises. Some plaintiffs have second thoughts or regrets about the future of their academic career, and some switch careers during or after the process. According to one anonymous plaintiff: "My case turned out fairly well, and I am at a point now that I would not be at had I not sued. However, I often think that if I really had it to do over again, I would choose a different career way back when I was in college."

Litigation frequently results in psychological and physical problems for plaintiffs. Kay Austen (see Chapter 2) suffered psychological stress, including bouts of depression and suicidal tendencies in her years-long conflict with her department chair and university administration. A decade of litigation also exacerbated a physical injury and left her permanently disabled. Other plaintiffs experience insomnia, ulcers, anxiety, panic attacks, violent headaches, "overwhelming tiredness," post-traumatic stress disorder, and other stress-related symptoms. Several plaintiffs seek professional counseling to help cope with the stress. Diana Paul, who did not personally experience physical ailments, noted that other plaintiffs' health declined during the litigation process. Paul says she was "careful to pay attention to my health and stress level" and maintain other activities and relationships so that the "litigation will not be all-consuming and potentially destructive. This is very important for physical and mental health."

Suing for sex discrimination in an academic context can be a consuming avocation that affects all aspects of a plaintiff's life. One plaintiff summarized: "The toll of pursuing such cases is extraordinary. There are few, if any, women who emerge uncompromised with respect to their health, their financial situation, or their professional life."

Given that a lawsuit can wreak havoc on so many aspects of a plaintiff's life, from her self-esteem to her financial outlook, one might conclude that litigation isn't worth it. In retrospect, some plaintiffs regretted their decision to sue. Janet Lever concluded that if she had it to do over she would not sue and would "get even by other ways, less damaging to my career and psyche."

Intangible Rewards

Yet plaintiffs' cumulative biography is decidedly not a cautionary tale against litigation. To the contrary, litigants often describe two things vividly and simultaneously: the profound challenges and frustrations that a lawsuit can bring and their commitment to the decision nonetheless. In many cases they aver that they would not have done anything differently, even with the benefit of hindsight, and that they have few, if any, regrets about their decision.

Why is this so? Some plaintiffs, of course, reach a favorable resolution through settlement, mediation, or court victories. These plaintiffs conclude that the struggles to achieve resolution are ultimately worth the cost. Even those who did not win the suit or who received no settlement, however, report having been transformed positively by the experience.

Plaintiffs do not typically interpret their primary motives as personal vindication or desire for financial gain. While these reasons may be important to plaintiffs, most see themselves as academic whistle-blowers who decide to take action to insist on fairness and justice for women and to change the academic culture. They envision their suit as beneficial for other women and a tool to expose what they perceive to be a discriminatory atmosphere or climate in their university or discipline. While the triggering incidents differ from person to person, the inspiration to continue with the suit typically comes from a broader commitment to women's rights in the academic community.

> *Most [plaintiffs] see themselves as academic whistle-blowers.*

Plaintiffs often describe their motivation in the language of justice and a quest to "do what's right." Anna Penk, lead plaintiff in the class-action suit described later in this chapter, was asked why she would risk an accomplished career for a sticky court battle. "Why are you living," she responded. "Why do you climb mountains. Why do you dance or listen to music. I feel as long as you're living, there's a lot of work to be done" (Hughes 1983, 3B).

Although citing litigation as "one of the most painful endeavors I have ever undertaken," an anonymous plaintiff also took comfort in having done the right thing by filing suit. Cynthia Fisher, who saw a half million dollar settlement in her favor reversed on appeal in a case described in Chapter 4, had no regrets about the lawsuit and "did not go into it expecting to win, and certainly not to win money." She initiated the suit because she and her lawyers felt she had an especially strong case of sex discrimination in academia, including that rarest of creatures—an absolute comparable male candidate whose record Fisher surpassed on most criteria.

Faith in the abstract virtue or rectitude of litigation may seem a small consolation, but it is at the core of many plaintiffs' initial impetus to go public with their case and their stamina throughout the arduous process. Purely individual goals for settlement, money, or retribution clearly would be insufficient to sustain the momentum through an often years-long legal odyssey against a well-resourced and tenacious university.

Some plaintiffs place themselves along a continuum of past and future female scholars. They feel a responsibility to defend the gains secured by their predecessors and promote the prospects for their successors, including their students. Catherine Clinger described her lawsuit as an effort to hold people accountable and responsible for their actions:

> I feel strongly that the higher education system is one that is quite reliant on academic advisors acting as mentors. . . . There are my students witnessing this [tenure denial] and . . . I was stalwart about the whole thing. I assured them that this wouldn't be the final assay, and, as they suspected, it was unjust and because it was, I would resist it. So I did. . . . I also wanted to honor what [my department colleagues] did for me—they had given me unanimous scores on my tenure application. Especially in the beginning, this was about justice and not individual justice. Then I was in my late 30s and I had accomplished so much for a woman. . . . I was operating with the benefit of having the mothers before and I was continuing the line.

Clinger summarized that while the litigation "took me to places I never truly desired to be," she felt that she is "better for it and for having really stuck to my position." Cynthia Fisher said, "Complacency is our worst enemy. . . . Younger women think we have won equal rights and many in the middle levels [of professions] have and may say, 'our mothers did our work and we're fine.' If we don't keep fighting we are going to lose [those rights].'"

Most plaintiffs file suit with an eye to institutional change. Some describe inertia within universities as the most disappointing outcome of their litigation. According to one plaintiff:

> The most dispiriting thing to me is that the successes (few as they are) do not seem to translate into improved status for women in general in the universities. In most instances, universities just go on with business as usual. Often, administrators and faculty who are sued for discrimination are even rewarded by promotions. . . . I think the advancement women have made in universities over the long range has been greater because women have spoken out, sued, and fought for every gain. . . . But the progress is depressingly slow.

Beth Kern found that in the end she wasn't as concerned about changing Notre Dame as she was at the outset of her suit: "My lawsuit wasn't Notre Dame's first discrimination suit; it probably won't be the last. A very wise person told me that a lawsuit won't change Notre Dame. Only substantial outside pressure, such as pressure from their donor base or public opinion, would motivate them to change. She told me that you [go through] this process for your self-respect. In the end she was quite right."

Complacency is our worst enemy.

Winning in the Court of Public Opinion

Despite these sobering comments, cases can spur significant institutional changes simply because they make the public aware of the problem. *Penk v. Oregon State Board of Higher Education* is a case in point. The class-action suit relied on statistical analysis to show disparities in pay and promotion between men and women. The board countered that sex-neutral factors could account for differences and argued that individual institutions within the state education system were the appropriate targets of legal action, not the board. U.S. District Court Judge Helen Frye concluded that no pattern or practice of discrimination existed of which the board should have been aware. Frye's ruling stunned Oregonians and others who had followed the case. Penk and her colleagues appealed to the 9th Circuit Court of Appeals and the Supreme Court and lost.

> *Cases can spur significant institutional changes simply because they make the public aware of the problem.*

Yet *Penk* was heard in the fabled court of public opinion as well as the courtroom proper. Editorials and op-eds sided with the *Penk* plaintiffs against the state university system. According to Elizabeth Lindeman Leonard, the *Willamette Week* ran a forceful editorial saying, "Faculty women of Oregon are and have been discriminated against. Anyone who took the trouble to attend the *Penk* trial would have been forced to come to the conclusion that the state system is riddled with sex discrimination at the faculty and administrative levels." The *Oregonian* concluded that although discrimination is difficult to find in a decentralized system, "the fact remains that 2,200 women faculty members throughout Oregon remain convinced they were discriminated against! The case will be a pyrrhic victory for the state unless hiring, pay and promotion procedures are changed so that women can compete on a level with their male colleagues" (Leonard 1986, 17).

State legislators were also impressed with the evidence heard in the case, and the Oregon legislature subsequently passed a law against discrimination in the state's institutions of higher education. The case also attracted the attention of California legislators, whose State Assembly Committee on Education held hearings on the tenure review process and its impact on women and minorities.

Publicity in such cases can benefit the plaintiff and female faculty because it gets the attention of legislators, advocates, and other organizations that can work toward long-term safeguards against sex discrimination and improvements in hiring and promotion. Thus, the plaintiff's personal battle is often one catalyst for change in a much longer process for universities.

Restoration

For many plaintiffs, the litigation process *restores* more than it takes away. Plaintiffs already experience one form of powerlessness—personal loss—as well as discrimination when the university makes its adverse employment decision. From this vantage point, the plaintiff's decision to tell her story to a grievance committee, the courts, or other audiences can restore a sense of respect and personal esteem. She imagines that a stance of passive acceptance or silence would be far more personally damaging than all of the challenges of litigation. As Kern summarized, "I let Notre Dame take away my self-respect while I was on its faculty. The litigation process restored it. That is priceless."

> *The litigation process restored [my self-respect]. That is priceless.*

Plaintiffs report that they gain things in unexpected ways and places through the process of appeal and litigation and the introspection that the dismissal and lawsuit stimulate. Some re-examine their fundamental career and life goals and find new professions and avocations. Some gain confidence from pursuing litigation, responding to detractors, dealing honestly with critics of their character and work, and speaking out openly about their experiences. Some discover new networks of support and friendship, and some confirm the strength of their family and friendships.

Plaintiffs may also find collegial support in unexpected places and gain a perspective that might otherwise have remained hidden. Beth Kern described the "unbelievably heartwarming" aftermath of her litigation. "My field, accountancy, tends to be conservative," she explained. "I was astounded by the number of people who contacted me once the matter was resolved. I received congratulatory comments from across the country."

The experiences described by these LAF-supported plaintiffs are a far cry from the stereotype of a frivolous lawsuit waged for personal gain. These women dedicated time and money to pursue what they saw as justice and equity. In the process, they subjected themselves to intense public scrutiny and criticism. Many became pariahs in their professional communities, straining some friendships and losing others. But regardless of the outcome, their cases force an examination of the employment policies and practices in academia and, in so doing, contribute to the broader struggle for gender equity in the workplace.

CHAPTER 6

Recommendations

To paraphrase Tolstoy, all happy departments in universities are happy in the same way, but all unhappy departments are unhappy in different ways. We do not hear much about functional, fair, and equitable academic departments because these departments do routine things correctly. They apply policies consistently, deliberate fairly on employment decisions, and take proactive steps to resolve faculty grievances before they ever reach the courts. Unhappy departments and tenure cases, on the other hand, are as variable and complex as the individuals and universities involved.

Plaintiffs supported by the AAUW Legal Advocacy Fund describe different triggers for a sex discrimination lawsuit—a hostile letter, inflammatory comments, a violation of tenure procedures, or perceived animus by a senior faculty member or administrator. Plaintiffs sense that they have been treated differently, and worse, than their colleagues. Ultimately, plaintiffs reach the same conclusion: In one form or another they have been discriminated against because of their sex.

A lawsuit should be a last resort. Legal action is an expensive and time-consuming process that can bring public embarrassment to one or both parties. The suggestions below are intended to help prevent litigation through informed faculty; sound, clearly articulated policies; and consistently applied practices.

Recommendations for Universities and Colleges

Good employment policies and practices go a long way. At a minimum, the tenure process should be consistent and clearly articulated. Procedural lapses create ill will and insecurity among faculty and invite suspicions of discrimination. For example, if the dean can reverse department recommendations, this should be made clear to incoming faculty. Specifically, university administrators and senior faculty should consider the following:

- **Design school policies that comply with antidiscrimination laws, and ensure that faculty and administrators understand and comply with those policies.**

- **Require annual written evaluations with explicit performance measures to address the candidate's progress in research, service, and teaching.** Base tenure decisions on concrete, measurable contributions rather than vague or inconsistent characterizations of "strong scholarship" or "excellent service." For example, scholarly productivity might be quantified within a department by having faculty clarify the relative weight assigned to particular journals in the tenure deliberations. Departments might also assess scholarly productivity through the number of times a work is cited in a positive manner. Such measures would lend some precision to the tenure process or, at a minimum, illustrate for tenure candidates where disagreements among the faculty exist.

- **Recognize the power tenured professors have over junior faculty and students and actively watch for and monitor abuses.** Set forth and enforce a range of consequences for offenders so that punishment will be meted out for all infractions, not just the most egregious. Several plaintiffs were dismayed that "serial harassers" were protected throughout their careers. A lack of consequences tacitly sanctions such behavior.

- **Take conflicts of interest in hiring or promotion seriously.** As one LAF-supported plaintiff puts it, having a close friend or old adviser on the search committee is the equivalent of "getting the answers before the test." If strong personal friendships or bonds between a candidate and a search committee member all but preselect the candidate, that committee member should not be in a sole or influential decision-making position.

- **Adopt a policy allowing for "time off the tenure clock" for childbirth and parenting.** Ensure that this policy fulfills requirements of the Family and Medical Leave Act as well as any other federal and state laws regarding pregnancy and the rights of new parents.
- **Treat rejected tenure candidates respectfully.** Avoid indignities or other small lapses in judgment that can become emotionally charged triggers for potential plaintiffs. A substantial number of LAF-supported plaintiffs report that the poor handling of their tenure decision, the careless or thoughtless way they were informed about the decision, or the university's reluctance to explain the decision honestly and diligently became emotionally significant final straws that pushed the plaintiffs further toward litigation. If the faculty and administration have deliberated fairly and with due diligence, they should explain their decision forthrightly and with respect for the candidate's dignity and professional contributions.
- **Offer services to support faculty as they seek new positions** so that a tenure denial does not become the end of the rejected candidate's academic career.
- **Provide written tenure policies and procedures to all faculty and prospective employees.** Several LAF-supported plaintiffs asserted that universities did not honor promises regarding tenure or promotion. Documenting all aspects of a job offer can help avoid a "she said, he said" disagreement.

Recommendations for Female Academics

One cannot always avoid becoming a victim of sex discrimination, but there are tactics for reducing one's risk as well as strategies for dealing with discrimination to avoid the financial and emotional costs of litigation. Steps taken before accepting a job and during the pre-tenure years can help women protect themselves against discrimination.

Before accepting a job offer

- **Ask for written information about the university's promotion and tenure policy,** including a description of recent tenure cases. Whenever possible, conduct these conversations by e-mail and save all correspondence.
- **Bear in mind that the chair of your department is likely to change before you are evaluated for tenure.** Recognize that the dean or other key players in the tenure process may change as well. Consider the likely scenarios for succession to these positions and what impact succession may have on you and your position.
- **Ask the department chair and other tenured faculty in your department what service, teaching, and scholarship will be needed for tenure and how your record will be weighed.** Request specific examples (e.g., which journals are considered top tier and how different accomplishments—books, articles, grants, other honors—are weighed). If you are considering a joint appointment, discuss how your contributions to both fields will be weighed in the tenure decision.

While on the job

- **Keep your antenna up for the culture and politics of your department and institution.** Observe and verse yourself in the unofficial practices. This informal culture may or may not correspond to formal, written policies, but it inevitably plays a role in hiring and promotion decisions. Some of your colleagues may also be your friends, but working relationships and job retention may trump friendship if you charge the institution with sex discrimination.
- **Cultivate friends, communities, and colleagues outside your department and outside academia.** Should you eventually find yourself in a dispute over salary, promotion, or tenure, these nonacademic sources of support will be especially sustaining and important.
- **Do not expect to be rewarded for doing favors or for being flexible.** Be a good team player, but document any special favors or concessions in writing.

- **In dire cases, consider cutting your losses early.** One plaintiff wishes that she had looked for another academic job as soon as she realized how women were treated in her department. In some cases, this may be the best pre-emptive course of action if you value a long-term academic career, given the difficulties of overcoming the "troublemaker" label once you have sued. By applying for other jobs before a tenure review, you may stand a good chance of getting recommendations and support from the department.
- **Understand your rights as an employee under federal and state law.** Many sources of information about employee rights are available, including the organizations listed in the selected resources appendix on page 87.
- **Immediately document any perceived discrimination.**

When a lawsuit is necessary

- **Carefully document conversations and actions that you take,** and save written materials that may be relevant to your case. Chronology is important.
- **Seek skilled mediators,** if possible, who might facilitate negotiations or resolution with the university early in the process, before litigation becomes the last resort.
- **Seek experienced legal counsel.** Personal rapport with an attorney is indeed critical, but it is not enough. As Catherine Clinger observed, a "true believer with a good heart is comforting but an experienced attorney with lots of knowledge is best. If you find both, great." To secure the best possible legal counsel, plaintiffs recommend that litigants ask several specific questions, including the following:
  - What experience does the attorney have in both civil rights law and faculty discrimination?
  - What is the attorney's track record in arguing or trying similar cases?
  - Does the attorney understand academia? One plaintiff commented, "It has been difficult trying to explain the nuances of tenure and review process" to her counsel.

- How does the attorney assess the "winnability" of the case?
- Does the attorney ask a lot of meaningful and logical questions about the case? Is she or he engaged in your narrative?
- Does the attorney have high visibility—which can be critical when suing universities that have prominence and deep roots in the community—and a good track record in lawsuits against large institutions?

- **Be realistic about the financial and emotional costs of litigation.** Talk to other plaintiffs who have pursued similar cases, and listen to their advice and words of caution.
- **Remember that publicity may help rather than hinder your case.** Although plaintiffs often tend to keep their potential lawsuit as quiet as possible in hopes of an early resolution or in fear that their actions will impede their job search, going public with the story has advantages. Consult legal counsel before consenting to publicity about your case.
- **Do not go through the process alone.** Almost all LAF-supported plaintiffs underscore that they could not have pursued litigation without the unfailing support of family, friends— inside and outside the academy—and other communities. Seek support from other organizations, individuals, and groups who understand the tenure process and support female plaintiffs. In addition to the AAUW Legal Advocacy Fund, plaintiffs in this study sought financial, technical, and emotional support from the American Association of University Professors, the National Women's Studies Association, local women's groups, and other organizations. See also the selected resources listed in Appendix B on page 87.

Appendix A

Tables

Table 1. Number and Percent of Doctoral Degrees Awarded by Race/Ethnicity and Gender, Academic Years 1980–81 and 2000–01

	1980–81		2000–01	
	Number	Percent	Number	Percent
All	31,106	100.0	40,744	100.0
Men	21,013	67.6	22,769	55.9
Women	10,093	32.4	17,901	43.9
Unreported			74	0.2
African American men	483	1.6	587	1.4
African American women	564	1.8	1,017	2.5
American Indian men	44	0.1	67	0.2
American Indian women	33	0.1	82	0.2
Asian American men	281	0.9	741	1.8
Asian American women	171	0.5	641	1.6
Hispanic men	344	1.1	497	1.2
Hispanic women	191	0.6	622	1.5
Non-U.S.-citizen men	4,536	14.6	7,980	19.6
Non-U.S.-citizen women	896	2.9	3,621	8.9
White, non-Hispanic men	13,987	45.0	11,257	27.6
White, non-Hispanic women	7,690	24.7	10,585	26.0
Unreported	1,886	6.1	3,047	7.5

Note. AAUW calculations based on Table 14 in William B. Harvey, *Minorities in Higher Education, 20th Annual Status Report, 2002–2003* (2003, 66). Original source: National Opinion Research Center at the University of Chicago, Doctorate records files, various years.

Table 2. Percentage of Full-time Faculty by Academic Rank and Gender, Academic Years 1981–82 to 1999–2000

	1981–82 Men	1981–82 Women	1999–2000 Men	1999–2000 Women
All full-time faculty	73.3	26.7	62.5	37.5
Full professor	89.7	10.3	79.1	20.9
Associate professor	79.2	20.8	64.5	35.5
Assistant professor	66.5	33.5	54.2	45.8
Instructor and lecturer	57.2	42.8	48.7	51.3
Other faculty	62.7	37.3	54.2	45.8

Note. AAUW calculations based on Table 29 in William B. Harvey, *Minorities in Higher Education, 20th Annual Status Report, 2002–2003* (2003, 90). Original source: U.S. Department of Education, National Center for Education Statistics, *Integrated Postsecondary Education System (IPEDS), Fall Staff Survey,* various years. (Participation in the IPEDS is required for institutions that participate in federal student loan programs such as Pell Grants or Stafford loans. Employment data is based on degree-granting institutions, including those offering four-year and two-year degrees.)

Table 3. Tenure Among Full-time Faculty at Title IV Degree-granting Institutions in the United States by Gender, Fall 2001

	4-year Number	4-year Percent	2-year Number	2-year Percent	Total Number	Total Percent
All faculty	498,286	100.0	119,582	100.0	617,868	100.0
Men	319,719	64.2	60,766	50.8	380,485	61.6
Women	178,567	35.8	58,816	49.2	237,383	38.4
Faculty with						
tenure	229,720	46.1	49,105	41.1	278,825	45.1
Men	167,496	72.9	25,825	52.6	193,321	69.3
Women	62,224	27.1	23,280	47.4	85,504	30.7
Percentage of male						
faculty with tenure		52.4		42.5		50.8
Percentage of women						
faculty with tenure		34.8		39.6		36.0

Note. Institutions include public, private nonprofit, and private for-profit schools that offer four-year or two-year degrees (U.S. Department of Education 2003, Table D, 6).

Table 4. Full-time Faculty by Academic Rank, Gender, and Selected Race/Ethnicity, Academic Years 1981–82 and 1999–2000

	1981–82		1999–2000	
	Number	Percent	Number	Percent
Full and Associate Professors				
All	220,794	100.0	286,612	100.0
African American men	4,006	1.8	6,679	2.3
African American women	1,966	0.9	4,567	1.6
American Indian men	336	0.2	585	0.2
American Indian women	212	0.1	280	0.1
Asian American men	6,256	2.8	13,384	4.7
Asian American women	765	0.3	3,154	1.1
Hispanic men	2,086	0.9	4,134	1.4
Hispanic women	518	0.2	1,940	0.7
White men	174,285	78.9	183,441	64.0
White women	30,364	13.8	68,448	23.9
Assistant Professors				
All	110,974	100.0	127,673	100.0
African American men	2,749	2.5	3,882	3.0
African American women	2,670	2.4	4,549	3.6
American Indian men	197	0.2	300	0.2
American Indian women	84	0.1	313	0.2
Asian American men	3,390	3.1	6,199	4.9
Asian American women	959	0.9	3,519	2.8
Hispanic men	1,204	1.1	2,291	1.8
Hispanic women	567	0.5	1,946	1.5
White men	66,270	59.7	56,463	44.2
White women	32,884	29.6	48,211	37.8

Note. White refers to white, non-Hispanic faculty only. Full and associate professors are usually tenured; assistant professors are usually not tenured. Most assistant professors are "tenure-track," which means that they are eligible to apply for tenure after some set period of time (usually five to seven years). AAUW calculations based on Table 29 in William B. Harvey, *Minorities in Higher Education, 20th Annual Status Report, 2002–2003* (2003, 90–92). Original source: U.S. Department of Education, National Center for Education Statistics, *Integrated Postsecondary Education System (IPEDS), Fall Staff Survey,* various years.

APPENDIX B

Selected Resources

AAUW Legal Advocacy Fund Phone: 202/785-7750
1111 16th St. N.W. TDD: 202/785-7777
Washington, DC 20036 Fax: 202/785-8754
E-mail: laf@aauw.org
www.aauw.org

The AAUW Legal Advocacy Fund is the nation's only legal fund focused solely on sex discrimination in higher education. Since 1981, LAF has helped students, faculty, staff, and administrators in higher education challenge discriminatory practices such as sexual harassment, denial of tenure or promotion, pay inequity, retaliation, and inequality in women's athletics programs. LAF provides financial support, a nationwide referral network of experienced lawyers and experts, and information about sex discrimination in higher education through outreach and public education efforts. It also rewards campus programs that demonstrate progress toward gender equity.

American Association of University Professors Phone: 202/737-5900
1012 14th St. N.W., Suite 500 Fax: 202/737-5526
Washington, DC 20005 www.aaup.org

The American Association of University Professors advances academic freedom and shared governance, defines fundamental professional values and standards for higher education, and ensures higher education's contribution to the common good. The AAUP Academic Freedom and Tenure Committee and the Committee on Women in the Academic Profession focus on issues of interest to women faculty. AAUP offers workshops, presentations, reports, the "Legal Watch" column, and legal support.

American Federation of Teachers Phone: 202/879-4400
555 New Jersey Ave. N.W. www.aft.org
Washington, DC 20001
The American Federation of Teachers works to improve the quality
of undergraduate education, forward issues of social justice, and make
education be about education and the unencumbered pursuit of
knowledge. AFT offers links to research on discrimination in higher
education, provides publications, organizes meetings and conferences,
and raises awareness of legislative issues.

Equal Rights Advocates Phone: 415/621-0672 or 800/839-4372
1663 Mission St., Suite 250 Fax: 415/621-6744
San Francisco, CA 94103 www.equalrights.org
Equal Rights Advocates strives to protect and secure equal rights and
economic opportunities for women through litigation and advocacy.
ERA focuses on employment sectors where gender discrimination is
pervasive and the potential to help women through legal advocacy is
high. ERA works to dismantle the barriers that prevent the full and
equal participation of women in higher education.

Legal Momentum Phone: 212/925-6635
395 Hudson St. Fax: 212/226-1066
New York, NY 10014 E-mail: peo@legalmomentum.org
www.legalmomentum.org
Formerly the NOW Legal Defense and Education Fund, Legal
Momentum advances the rights of women and girls by using the
power of the law and creating innovative public policy. Its work
focuses on three broad initiatives: economic justice, freedom from
gender-based violence, and equality under the law.

National Education Association Phone: 202/833-4000
1201 16th St. N.W. Fax: 202/822-7974
Washington, DC 20036-3290 www.nea.org
The National Education Association has a long history as the
nation's leading organization committed to advancing the cause of
public education. NEA provides publications, leadership tools,
professional advisers, online teaching and learning resources, a higher

education research center, and conferences to promote the cause of equality in education.

National Employment Lawyers Association Phone: 415/296-7629
44 Montgomery St., Suite 2080 Fax: 415/677-9445
San Francisco, CA 94104 www.nela.org

The National Employment Lawyers Association is the country's only professional organization exclusively comprised of lawyers who represent individual employees in cases involving employment discrimination, wrongful termination, employee benefits, and other employment related matters. NELA strives to promote workplace fairness by offering networking, educational programs, publications, and membership benefits such as a brief bank.

National Partnership for Women & Families Phone: 202/986-2600
1875 Connecticut Ave. N.W., Suite 650 Fax: 202/986-2539
Washington, DC 20009 E-mail: info@nationalpartnership.org
www.nationalpartnership.org

A nonprofit, nonpartisan organization, the National Partnership for Women & Families uses public education and advocacy to promote fairness in the workplace, quality health care, and policies that help women and men meet the dual demands of work and family.

National Women's Law Center Phone: 202/588-5180
11 Dupont Cir. N.W., Suite 800 Fax: 202/588-5185
Washington, DC 20036 www.nwlc.org

The National Women's Law Center is a nonprofit legal advocacy organization dedicated to the advancement and protection of women's rights and the elimination of sex discrimination from all facets of life. Priority areas include education, employment, family economic security, and health.

U.S. Department of Education Phone: 800/421-3481
Office for Civil Rights TDD: 877/521-2172
Customer Service Team Fax: 202/245-6840
550 12th St. S.W. E-mail: ocr@ed.gov
Washington, DC 20202-1100 www.ed.gov/about/offices/list/ocr/index.html

The Office for Civil Rights works to ensure equal access to education and promotes educational excellence throughout the nation through vigorous enforcement of civil rights.

U.S. Department of Justice
Civil Rights Division
Employment Litigation Section, PHB
950 Pennsylvania Ave. N.W.
Washington, DC 20530

Phone: 202/514-3831
Fax: 202/514-1005 or 1105
www.usdoj.gov/crt/

The Employment Litigation Section enforces Title VII of the Civil Rights Act of 1964 against state and local government employers. The section challenges discriminatory employment practices that cause unlawful disparate impact and disparate treatment. The section also issues right-to-sue notices to individuals who have filed EEOC charges against state and local government employers.

U.S. Department of Labor
Office of Federal Contract Compliance Programs
200 Constitution Ave. N.W.
Washington, DC 20210

www.dol.gov

The Office of Federal Contract Compliance Programs enforces Executive Order 11246, which prohibits discrimination in hiring or employment on the basis of race, color, gender, religion, and national origin. The OFCCP investigates complaints of discrimination, grants awards, offers employers guidance on how to pay equally and fairly, lists employment opportunities, and provides a partnership website.

U.S. Equal Employment Opportunity Commission
1801 L St. N.W.
Washington, DC 20507

www.eeoc.gov

Through mediation and litigation, the Equal Employment Opportunity Commission enforces federal laws that prohibit discrimination in the workplace on the basis of race, sex, religion, age, and disability. The EEOC investigates charges of discrimination; provides guidance on discrimination laws; and offers outreach and education programs, technical assistance and training programs, seminars, and publications.

APPENDIX C

Cited Tenure Cases Supported by the AAUW Legal Advocacy Fund

References

Cases and Legal Sources

Austen v. State of Hawaii, 759 F. Supp. 612 (D. Haw. 1991), *affirmed*, 967 F.2d 583 (9th Cir. 1992).

Bickerstaff v. Vassar College, 992 F. Supp. 372 (S.D.N.Y. 1998).

Brown v. Trustees of Boston University, 891 F.2d 337 (1st Cir. 1989).

Campbell v. Ramsay, 631 F.2d 597 (8th Cir. 1980).

Civil Rights Act of 1991, 42 U.S.C. § 1981.

Crystal, Jill. 1993. *Grievance before the Grievance Review Board*. University of Michigan, Ann Arbor College of Literature, Science, and the Arts.

Davis v. Weidner, 596 F.2d 726 (7th Cir. 1979).

Delaware State College v. Ricks, 449 U.S. 250 (1980).

Faro v. New York University, 502 F.2d 1229 (2d Cir. 1974).

Fields v. Clark University, Civ. No. 80-1011-S, 1986 WL 5350 (D. Mass. March 14, 1986), *vacated and remanded*, 817 F.2d 931 (1st Cir. 1987), 1991 WL 349620 (D. Mass. April 16, 1991), *affirmed*, 966 F.2d 49 (1st Cir. 1992), *certiorari denied*, 506 U.S. 1052 (1993).

————, Memorandum of defendant Clark University in support of its motion to dismiss the complaint, U.S. Dist. Ct., Dist. of Mass., Civil Action No. 80-1011-K (December 27, 1990).

————, Transcript of non-jury trial (Day 3), U.S. Dist. Ct., Dist. of Mass., Civil Action No. 80-1011-K (December 21, 1990).

————, Transcript of non-jury trial (Day 4), U.S. Dist. Ct., Dist. of Mass., Civil Action No. 80-1011-K (January 25, 1991).

Fisher v. Vassar College, 852 F. Supp. 1193 (S.D.N.Y. 1994), *affirmed in part and vacated in part,* 70 F.3d 1420 (2d Cir. 1995), *affirmed en banc,* 114 F.3d 1332 (2d Cir. 1997), *certiorari denied,* 522 U.S. 1075 (1998).

Goltz, Sonia, and Beth B. Kern, *Discrimination all women face at the College of Business at the University of Notre Dame,* U.S. Equal Employment Opportunity Commission, Indianapolis, Ind., Charge No. 240940156 (October 4, 1993).

Griggs v. Duke Power Company, 401 U.S. 424 (1971).

Ilon v. State University of New York, Buffalo, Complaint, State of N.Y., County of Niagara Supreme Ct., No. 107009 (November 27, 2000).

Lever v. Northwestern University, No. 84C11025, 1991 WL 206066 (N.D. Ill. October 4, 1991), *affirmed,* 979 F.2d 552 (7th Cir. 1992), *certiorari denied* 508 U.S. 951 (1993).

Lovell v. University of California, Berkeley, Complaint, Superior Ct. of the State of Cal., County of Alameda, Case No. 667157-4 (June 28, 1990).

Lynn v. Regents of University of California, 656 F.2d 1337 (9th Cir. 1981).

Margolis v. Williams College, Answer, Massachusetts Commission Against Discrimination, Action No. 84-SEM-0112 (February 10, 1987).

————, Petitioner's memorandum in support of her motion to compel production of documents, Massachusetts Commission Against Discrimination, Action No. 84-SEM-0112 (n.d.).

Mayberry v. Dees, 663 F.2d 502 (4th Cir. 1981).

McDonnell Douglas Corporation v. Green, 411 U.S. 792 (1973).

Miller v. Texas Tech University Health Sciences Center, Complaint, U.S. Dist. Ct., Northern Dist. of Tex., Case No. 2-00CV-0364J (November 3, 2000).

Paul v. Stanford University, No. C-84-20652-RPA, 1986 WL 614 (N.D. Cal. January 23, 1986).

————, Declaration of Diana Paul in support of plaintiff's reply memorandum re motion to compel, Exhibit B, U.S. Dist. Ct., Northern Dist. of Cal., Case No. 84-20652 RPA (January 6, 1986).

Penk v. Oregon State Board of Higher Education, Civ. No. 80-436, 1985 WL 25631 (D. Ore. February 13, 1985), affirmed, 816 F.2d 458 (9th Cir. 1987), certiorari denied, 484 U.S. 853 (1987).

Price Waterhouse v. Hopkins, 490 U.S. 228 (1989).

Scott v. University of Delaware, 455 F. Supp. 1102 (D. Del. 1978).

St. Mary's Honor Center v. Hicks, 509 U.S. 502 (1993).

Stein v. Kent State University Board of Trustees, 994 F. Supp. 898 (N.D. Ohio 1998).

Sweezy v. State of New Hampshire by Wyman, 354 U.S. 234 (1957).

Texas Department of Community Affairs v. Burdine, 450 U.S. 248 (1981).

Title VII of the Civil Rights Act of 1964, 42 U.S.C. § 2000e et seq.

Title IX of the Education Amendments of 1972, 20 U.S.C. § 1681 et seq.

University of Pennsylvania v. EEOC, 493 U.S. 182 (1990).

Weinstock v. Columbia University, No. 95-Civ. 0569 (JFK), 1999 WL 549006 (S.D.N.Y. July 28, 1999), affirmed, 224 F.3d 33 (2d Cir. 2000), certiorari denied, 124 S. Ct. 53 (2003).

Zahorik v. Cornell University, 579 F. Supp. 349 (N.D.N.Y. 1983), affirmed, 729 F.2d 85 (2d Cir. 1984).

Other Sources

American Association of University Professors. 1988. Academic freedom and tenure: University of Judaism (California). Academe (May–June): 23–29.

————. 1999. New Mexico Highlands University: A case of denial of tenure. Academe 85 (2): 99–108. Retrieved August 31, 2004, from www.aaup.org/publications/Academe/1999/99ma/MA99nmhu.htm.

American Association of University Professors and Association of American Colleges. *1940 statement of principles on academic freedom and tenure with 1970 interpretive comments.* Washington, DC. Retrieved August 31, 2004, from www.aaup.org/statements/Redbook/1940stat.htm.

Cooper, Christine Godsil. 1983. Title VII in the academy: Barriers to equality for faculty women. *University of California Davis Law Review* 16: 975–1022.

Fosmoe, Margaret. 1998. Trial looms: Was N.D. business school sex-biased? *South Bend Tribune* (August 9): A1.

Harvey, William B. 2003. *Minorities in higher education: 20th annual status report, 2002–2003.* Washington, DC: American Council on Education.

Heline, Marti Goodlad. 1998. Notre Dame faces share of bias suits. *South Bend Tribune* (July 19): D1.

Hoffer, Thomas B., Scott Sederstrom, Lance Selfa, Vince Welch, Mary Hess, Shana Brown, Sergio Reyes, Kristy Webber, and Isabel Guzman-Barron. 2003. *Doctorate recipients from United States Universities: Summary report 2002.* Chicago: National Opinion Research Center at the University of Chicago.

Hughes, Richard. 1983. Suit cancels leisure time. *Statesman-Journal* (September 17): 1B, 3B.

Leonard, Elizabeth Lindeman. 1986. Faculty women for equity: A class-action suit against the State of Oregon. *Affilia* (Summer): 6–19.

Lewin, Tamar. 2002. "Collegiality" as a tenure battleground. *New York Times* (July 12).

Livingston, Jacqueline. 1985. The end of a dream. *Cornell Daily Sun* (February 14): 5.

Lovell, Margaretta M. 1990. *Testimony submitted to the California Assembly Committee on Education in conjunction with the hearing* [on the tenure review process and its impact on women and minorities] held October 30, in San Francisco.

Magner, Denise K. 1997. U. of Michigan at Dearborn revises its new tenure policy. *Chronicle of Higher Education* (October 31): A14.

Mahony, Ieuan G. 1987. Title VII and academic freedom: The authority of the EEOC to investigate college faculty tenure decisions. *Boston College Law Review* 28: 559–594.

Mangels, John. 2000. CWRU's fishy business. *Plain Dealer Sunday Magazine* (October 8): 12–18, 22.

———. 2001. Tenure based on gender, prof says. *Plain Dealer* (April 17): A5.

Rhodes responds to "Cornell 11" petition. 1981. *Cornell Chronicle* (December 3): 1.

Smallwood, Scott. 2001. Thorny tenure case at Case Western leads to sex-bias charges. *Chronicle of Higher Education* (February 23): A14–A17.

U.S. Department of Education, National Center for Education Statistics. 2002. *Digest of education statistics, 2002.* Washington, DC. Retrieved August 31, 2004, from nces.ed.gov/programs/digest/d02/.

———. 2003. *Staff in postsecondary institutions, Fall 2001, and salaries of full-time instructional faculty, 2001–02.* Washington, DC. (NCES Number 2004159). Retrieved August 31, 2004, from nces.ed.gov/pubsearch/pubsinfo.asp?pubid=2004159.

West, Martha. 1994. Gender bias in academic robes: The law's failure to protect women faculty. *Temple Law Review* 67: 67–139.

Wilson, Robin. 1997. Women lose tenure bids despite backing from departments. *Chronicle of Higher Education* (June 6): A10.

AAUW Gender Equity Library

Beyond the "Gender Wars": A Conversation About Girls, Boys, and Education
Report of the key insights presented during a symposium convened by the AAUW Educational Foundation in September 2000 to foster a discussion among scholars who study both girls' and boys' experiences in and out of school. Participants share their insights about gender identity and difference, challenge popular views of girls' and boys' behavior, and explore the meaning of equitable education for the 21st century.
AS49 ■ 60 pages/2001 ■ $9.95

Gaining a Foothold: Women's Transitions Through Work and College
Examines how and why women make changes in their lives through education. Profiles three groups—women going from high school to college, from high school to work, and from work to college—using qualitative and quantitative methods. Findings include an analysis of women's educational decisions, aspirations, and barriers.
AS37 ■ 100 pages/1999 ■ $6.49

Gender Gaps: Where Schools Still Fail Our Children
Measures schools' mixed progress toward gender equity and excellence since the 1992 publication of *How Schools Shortchange Girls: The AAUW Report*. Research compares student course enrollments, tests, grades, risks, and resiliency by race and class as well as gender. It finds some gains in girls' achievement, some areas where boys—not girls—lag, and some areas, like technology, where needs have not yet been addressed.
AS35 ■ 150 pages/1998 ■ $6.99
Executive Summary
AS36 ■ 24 pages/1998 ■ $3.99

Published by the AAUW Educational Foundation unless otherwise noted.

Girls in the Middle: Working to Succeed in School

Engaging study of middle school girls and the strategies they use to meet the challenges of adolescence. Report links girls' success to school reforms like team teaching and cooperative learning, especially where these are used to address gender issues.

AS29 ▪ 128 pages/1996 ▪ $7.49

Growing Smart: What's Working for Girls in School

Comprehensive academic review of more than 500 reports identifies approaches that promote girls' achievement and healthy development. Culturally conscious report urges experimentation with single-sex programs, cooperative learning, and other nontraditional approaches.

AS26 ▪ 97 pages/1995 ▪ $14.50
Executive Summary and Action Guide
AS25 ▪ 48 pages/1995 ▪ $6.49

Hostile Hallways: Bullying, Teasing, and Sexual Harassment in School (2001)

One student in five fears being hurt or bothered in school; four students in five personally experience sexual harassment. These are among the findings of this nationally representative survey of 2,064 eighth- through 11th-graders. The report investigates sexual harassment in public schools, comparing the findings with AAUW's original survey in 1993 and exploring differences in responses by gender, race/ethnicity, grade level, and area (urban or suburban/rural). Conducted by Harris Interactive.

AS50 ▪ 56 pages/2001 ▪ $9.95

Hostile Hallways: The AAUW Survey on Sexual Harassment in America's Schools (1993)

The first national study of sexual harassment in public schools. Includes gender and racial/ethnic data breakdowns. Conducted by Louis Harris and Associates.

AS17 ▪ 28 pages/1993 ▪ $5.99

How Schools Shortchange Girls: The AAUW Report

A startling examination of how girls are disadvantaged in U.S. public schools. Includes recommendations for educators and policy-makers as well as concrete strategies for change.

AS22 ▪ 224 pages/Marlowe, 1995 ▪ $6.49
Executive Summary
AS14 ▪ 8 pages/1992 ▪ $2.50

A License for Bias: Sex Discrimination, Schools, and Title IX
Examines uneven efforts to implement the 1972 civil rights law that protects some 70 million students and employees from sex discrimination in schools and universities.
AS48 ▪ 84 pages/AAUW Legal Advocacy Fund, 2000 ▪ $12.95

SchoolGirls: Young Women, Self-Esteem, and the Confidence Gap
Riveting book by journalist Peggy Orenstein in association with AAUW shows how girls in two racially and economically diverse California communities suffer the painful plunge in self-esteem documented in *Shortchanging Girls, Shortchanging America*.
AS27 ▪ 384 pages/Doubleday, 1994 ▪ $12.95

Separated by Sex: A Critical Look at Single-Sex Education for Girls
The foremost educational scholars on single-sex education in grades K-12 compare findings on whether girls learn better apart from boys. The report, including a literature review and a summary of a forum convened by the AAUW Educational Foundation, challenges the popular idea that single-sex education is better for girls.
AS34 ▪ 99 pages/1998 ▪ $12.95

Shortchanging Girls, Shortchanging America Executive Summary
Summary of the 1991 poll that assesses self-esteem, educational experiences, and career aspirations of girls and boys ages 9 through 15. Revised edition reviews poll's impact, offers action strategies, and highlights survey results with charts and graphs.
AS20 ▪ 20 pages/AAUW, 1994 ▪ $5.99

¡Sí, Se Puede! Yes, We Can: Latinas in School
Comprehensive look at the status of Latina girls in the U.S. public education system. Explores conflicts between institutional expectations and the realities of student lives and discusses the social, cultural, and community factors that affect Hispanic education.
AS46 (English) ▪ 84 pages/2001 ▪ $12.95
AS47 (Spanish) ▪ 90 pages/2001 ▪ $12.95

Tech-Savvy: Educating Girls in the New Computer Age
Explores girls' and teachers' perspectives on today's computer culture and technology use at school, home, and work. Presents recommendations for broadening access to computers for girls and others who don't fit the "male hacker/computer geek" stereotype.
AS45 ▪ 84 pages/2000 ▪ $12.95

Tenure Denied: Cases of Sex Discrimination in Academia

A collaborative research project of the AAUW Educational Foundation and the AAUW Legal Advocacy Fund, this report gives a human voice to the concept of sex discrimination and the struggles that female faculty face in academia.

EF003 ■ 105 pages/2004 ■ $10

The Third Shift: Women Learning Online

Through distance education, technology offers new opportunities for women to achieve educational goals. This report explores why women pursue education; how they balance work, family, and education; and what would make distance learning easier for them. Includes recommendations for improvements.

AS51 ■ 80 pages/2001 ■ $9.95

Under the Microscope: A Decade of Gender Equity Projects in the Sciences

Examines and analyzes more than 400 gender equity projects specifically aimed at increasing the participation of girls and women in science, technology, engineering, and mathematics (STEM). Reveals trends in the development and support of these projects during the last decade and offers recommendations for strengthening the advancement of gender equity in the sciences for the future.

EF002 ■ 40 pages ■ $12

Voices of a Generation: Teenage Girls on Sex, School, and Self

Compares the comments of roughly 2,100 girls nationwide on peer pressure, sexuality, the media, and school. The girls participated in AAUW teen forums called Sister-to-Sister Summits. The report explores differences by race, ethnicity, and age and offers the girls' action proposals to solve common problems.

AS39 ■ 95 pages/1999 ■ $7.50

Women at Work

Combines interview and survey data with recent U.S. census statistics to explore how women are faring in today's work force and what their prospects are for future job success and security.

AS55 ■ Report ■ 56 pages/2003 ■ $15.95
AS56 ■ Action Guide ■ 20 pages/2003 ■ $6.95
AS57 ■ Set (Report and Action Guide) ■ $19.95

ShopAAUW Order Form

Today's date ____/____/____

Join AAUW today and receive a 10% discount. Complete the new member box* below.

AAUW membership # (if applicable) _____

Name _____

Organization _____

Address (no P.O. Box) _____

City _____ State_____ ZIP _____

Daytime phone (____)_____ E-mail _____

METHOD OF PAYMENT
Make check or money order payable to Metro Graphic Communications. Do not send cash.

❏ Check/money order in the amount of $ _____

❏ MasterCard ❏ VISA ❏ AMERICAN EXPRESS ____ ____ - ____ ____ ____ - ____ ____ - ____ ____

Name on card _____

Expiration date _____

Signature _____

telephone orders
800/225-9998
ext. 558

fax orders
301/948-6233

online orders
www.aauw.org

Send completed form
and payment to
Metro Graphic Communications
P.O. Box 7410
Gaithersburg, MD
20898-7410

Qty	Item No	Item Description	Size	Unit Price

*New Members-at-Large ($42 for 2004–05)

College/University_____

State/Campus _____

Year/Degree_____

To join a local branch, call 800/326-AAUW
or visit www.aauw.org

**Sales Tax
Add sales tax for the following states:

DC–5.75%	NC–7.00%
MD–5.00%	VA–5.00%

***Shipping Charges

Shipping charges based on order size as follows:

Up to $24.99	$5.50
$25.00–$49.99	$7.00
$50.00–$74.99	$8.00
$75.00–$99.99	$10.50
$100.00–$149.99	$15.50
$150.00–$300.00	$18.00
Over $300.00	7% of order

All orders shipped UPS ground. For special shipping or shipments outside the U. S., please call for a quote.

SUBTOTAL	
10% Member Discount	
*AAUW Membership-at-Large ($42)	
TOTAL	
**Sales Tax (see table)	
Handling	3.50
***Shipping Charges (see table)	
TOTAL DUE	

SATISFACTION GUARANTEED. If you are not completely satisfied with your purchase, please return it in its original condition within 90 days for exchange, credit, or refund.

Prices are subject to change. Metro Graphic Communications Inc. Federal ID #52-0964217

For bulk pricing on orders of 10 or more publications, call 800/225-9998.

We Need Your Help . . .
Because Equity Is Still an Issue

The AAUW Educational Foundation and the AAUW Legal Advocacy Fund together form a powerful force working to improve the climate for women in education. The Educational Foundation's research on gender equity issues raises public awareness and provides a call to action for policy-makers and legislators. The Legal Advocacy Fund works to hold higher education institutions accountable for violations of the laws protecting women from sex discrimination on campus.

This work would not be possible without generous contributions from people like you. Our supporters share a commitment to education, a passion for equity, and an unwavering belief that women are an instrumental part of leadership, change, and growth. Your support of the AAUW Educational Foundation will ensure its ability to continue the groundbreaking research and scholarship that has helped bring the issues of women and girls to the forefront. Your support of the AAUW Legal Advocacy Fund will help campus women fight sexual harassment, pay inequity, and unfair tenure or promotion denials.

We need your help. Please give today!

❏ **Yes!** *I want to help improve the climate for women in education.*
Please accept my contribution of
  ❏ $250 ❏ $100 ❏ $50 ❏ $35 ❏ Other (specify_____)
Use this contribution as follows:
  _____ (indicate percent) to support the work of the
    AAUW Educational Foundation
  _____ (indicate percent) to help the AAUW Legal Advocacy
    Fund fight discrimination in higher education

Name _____

Address_____

City_____ State_____ ZIP _____

Daytime telephone_____

E-mail address _____

PAYMENT METHOD
❏ Check or money order payable to AAUW
❏ Credit card (check one) ❏ MasterCard ❏ VISA
Card no. ___ ___ ___ ___ ___ ___ ___ ___ ___ ___ ___ ___ ___ ___ ___ ___

Exp. date_____ Today's date _____

Name on card_____

Billing address ❏ Same as above

Address_____

City_____ State_____ ZIP _____

❏ Please send me information on how to include the Educational
Foundation or Legal Advocacy Fund in my will or trust.

Fax your completed form to 202/463-7169 or mail it to
    AAUW Development Office
    1111 Sixteenth St. N.W.
    Washington, DC 20036

To learn more about AAUW or to make contributions on the web,
visit www.aauw.org.

The AAUW Educational Foundation and AAUW Legal Advocacy Fund are
501(c)(3) corporations. Gifts are fully tax-deductible to the extent allowed by law.

The AAUW Educational Foundation provides funds to advance education, research, and self-development for women and to foster equity and positive societal change.

The AAUW Legal Advocacy Fund provides funding and a support system for women seeking judicial redress for sex discrimination.

In principle and in practice, the AAUW Educational Foundation and the AAUW Legal Advocacy Fund value and support diversity. There shall be no barriers to full participation in these organizations on the basis of gender, race, creed, age, sexual orientation, national origin, disability, or class.